S0-BOK-503

STRAVINSKY:

Classic Humanist

Da Capo Press Music Reprint Series

STRAVINSKY:

Classic Humanist

BY
HEINRICH STROBEL

Translated from the German by Hans Rosenwald

DA CAPO PRESS • NEW YORK • 1973

Library of Congress Cataloging in Publication Data

Strobel, Heinrich, 1898-
    Stravinsky: classic humanist.

    (Da Capo Press music reprint series)
    Reprint of the ed. published by Merlin Press, New
York, which was issued as v. 3 of Merlin music books.
    1. Stravinskii, Igor' Fedorovich, 1882-1971.
I. Title.
[ML410.S932S92   1973]   780'.92'4   73-4338
ISBN 0-306-70580-X

ML
410
.S932
.S92

This Da Capo Press edition of *Stravinsky: Classic Humanist*
is an unabridged republication of the 1955 edition
published in New York.

Copyright © 1955 by Merlin Press, Inc.

Published by Da Capo Press, Inc.
A Subsidiary of Plenum Publishing Corporation
227 West 17th Street, New York, N.Y. 10011

All Rights Reserved

Manufactured in the United States of America

STRAVINSKY:

Classic Humanist

STRAVINSKY:

Classic Humanist

HEINRICH STROBEL

Translated from the German

by Hans Rosenwald

MERLIN PRESS - NEW YORK

Copyright 1955. Merlin Press, Inc.

Manufactured in the United States of America.

THIS IS A MERLIN PRESS BOOK

OF THIS EDITION ONLY FIFTEEN HUNDRED
COPIES WERE MADE

THIS IS NUMBER ....

STRAVINSKY:

Classic Humanist

ITH THE RISE OF romanticism at the beginning of the nineteenth century a fundamental change occured in the relationship of the composer to his environment. Up to that time he had been subjected to a higher order determined by church and nobility. Commissioned by these agencies, he had created his works for the praise of God or that of his aristocratic patron, often not only a "lover" but also a "connoisseur" of the "science" of music. The subject matter of music, just as that of painting, remained fixed, with each epoch creating its own conventions and formulae for artistic realization. Therefore differentiations but of style exist between the late Gothic music of the fifteenth century and the Baroque of the eighteenth. Intellectual and sociological attitudes of these periods are identical. At all times individuality was subjugated to a superior order accepted without question.

This picture changed with the French Revolution. As the **tiers état** and the masses threw off the moral and social suppression of the **ancien régime,** the artistic personality, too, was freed from hitherto imposed conventions and formulae. Musical confession emerged from musical "science" subjected to a higher order: it was the confession of the creative individual. The musician begins to describe in tones his joy and suffering, his inner struggle and victory. No longer is he the servant of a class or society. He conquers the new **bourgeoisie** through the power of his individuality. His artistic message becomes a decisive element of the arts. Beethoven is the first and at the same time the most magnificent representative of this new concept in music.

In the shadow of this great master who knew how to amalgamate individuality and the science of music, expressiveness and construction in a unique fashion, the "blue flower" of romanticism began to blossom. How wholesome, beautiful and touching is the scent of this flower in the works of Schubert, Weber and Schumann! This is the intoxicating song of "love's sorrow and joy" in lovely vales as well as in tempest-torn canyons of nature re-discovered. But the **décor** rapidly changed and the "blue flower" of romanticism no longer grew on silent banks of meadows and beside friendly, rustling rivulets; instead it grew in the soul of the musician, a flower nurtured not by fresh springs, but by the heart's blood of the artist.

It is but a step from Weber's naive **Freischuetz** to the self-torturing phantasmagoria of Berlioz' **Symphonie Fantastique** from which, in turn, a straight road leads to Wagner's **Tristan und Isolde,** the very culmination, and at the same time the turning point, of the romanticism of music. Why culmination? Because never before had the musician expressed in tones his most personal experiences in such a grandiose manner, a manner wherein music, word and gesture penetrate each other in an unprecedented fashion; never before had musical expressiveness obtained such diversity and differentiation, and never before had the triumph of the creative individual been so overwhelmingly demonstrated. Why turning point? Because never before had tonality been pushed as far beyond its confines (which had been fixed, apparently with finality, at least for one century by Jean Philippe Rameau) as in Wagner's **Tristan;** never before had the chromatic scale of twelve half-steps gained such power in any musical **oeuvre.** Even Wagner became dizzy. In **Meistersinger** and in **Parsifal** he consciously returned to the old tonality.

The assault had succeeded. What had been considered eternal and untouchable, the major-minor tonality, now was shaken by an overwhelming onslaught of musical expressiveness, by an urge awakened in Richard Wagner's artistic soul as the result of his experience with Mathilde Wesendonck. The musicians with greatest fascination seized the opportunities which a new freedom promised them. They penetrated by means of tones ever more deeply into the mysteries of the human soul.

Piano and chamber music, once the bearers of musical romanticism, were fast pushed aside by the ever-growing orchestra. The language of the instruments suddenly attained unanticipated splendor and differentiation. **Salome** and **Elektra** by Richard Strauss, the symphonies of Gustav Mahler, wavering as they do between the longing for lost innocence and the composer's own emotional tortures, and Alban Berg's **Wozzeck** upset the listeners yesterday only to convert them tomorrow. What, then, had happened to that innocent **fleur bleue** of romanticism? It had turned into a **fleur du mal.** It was indeed an intoxicating flower; it glistened in a thousand colors, it was sensuous and bewildering with its death-laden scent.

In Vienna lived Arnold Schoenberg, a

composer who had given himself over to the musical expressionism of the late German romanticists with all the fibres of his heart, and had pushed expression to the last limits of death hysteria in his **Erwartung** and **Glueckliche Hand.** But he soon had to recognize that the excessiveness of expressive and sonorous means must end. Consequently he returned to scoring in the manner of chamber music, in truly novel combinations of instruments, and at the same time he abandoned the very limitations imposed upon the creative spirit by tonality. With his incomparable intellectual and creative intensity, Schoenberg, in the works composed shortly before World War I, pushed toward the free use of twelve half-steps within one octave of the tempered system.

One spoke of "atonal" music in those days, a term which Schoenberg himself strongly repudiated. He recognized within a short time, however, that the uncontrolled operation with twelve half-steps would lead to an arbitrariness that could constitute real danger to music itself. How great such danger could be was convincingly proved by the so-called "New Music" prevailing in the Middle Europe of the twenties. After long search Schoenberg found, during a rest period in his creativeness, a new order: the order of the **Reihe,** the series. It meant that he selected for every work a series of twelve tones of the chromatic scale which, in four variations, is obligatory for the composition in question, horizontally as well as vertically.

Schoenberg followed his new order at first with that inexorable severity which is an integral part of his personality. Later, when he had emigrated to the United States, he allowed certain modifi-

12

cations in favor of the old tonality, without touching, however, the principle of his discovery. This modification, stylistically speaking a certain "creative relaxation," goes hand in hand with his references—that can scarcely be overlooked —to Bach and Brahms. Now the historic cycle was completed. Schoenberg stands at the end of the post-romantic German movement epitomized in expressionism; at the same time he represents the beginning of a new epoch.

Two devoted friends and disciples, Alban Berg and Anton von Webern, even during Schoenberg's lifetime developed different aspects of twelve-tone music. Both were followers of a master whose discovery by its very nature had to remain strongly theoretical. Berg was of a more lyrical and poetic nature. One can see in him the impressionist height of twelve-tone music. Webern turned to completely different paths and, by means of his dodecaphonic workmanship, founded a new style which combines utmost abstraction with unprecedented sensitivity to sonority.

The structural dissolution of romantic music into small fragments of sound, thematically and rhythmically no longer interrelated, but epitomized in expressiveness, obtains its highest degree in Webern's work. Webern's music, at first considered drily theoretical, in reality is replete with many emotional implications and exercises a most profound effect on our younger generation of composers. Through him the mysterious realms of psychoanalysis were opened up to music, the realms of a science whose discoverer, Siegmund Freud, also hails from Vienna —certainly no coincidence!

The tendencies toward over-refinement and abstraction in the expressionist movement in the later romantic era, the school of Schoenberg, of necessity produced a reaction. This reaction, represented in Germany by the young Paul Hindemith and in France by **Les Six,** a group working under the influence of the very strange Erik Satie, is personified in the Eastern countries by Igor Stravinsky and Bela Bartok. Different as their national idioms may be, they all have one thing in common: a new rhythmic and melodic vitality. The blue flower of romanticism had become the object of scientific experimentation. The earthy and elemental powers of music rise again as reaction to such experiments. Too long had rhythm been pushed aside—all too long—by the romanticists whose orientation towards harmony was indeed one-sided. As a matter of fact, rhythm's manifold possibilities and combinations had not even been considered by most Euro-

pean musicians. The French were enthralled by the dance music which had invaded their country from abroad. Eastern
composers discovered the elemental substance of folk music now freed from
romantic trappings and some enjoyed
more, some less a new freedom of harmonic thinking brought about by Schoenberg.

That was the widely hailed epoch of
"New Music." Fresh blood flowed into
the veins of a body calcified by German
symphonism. Substances rich in vita-
mins strengthened music's fatigued
bones. A healthy creative optimism
united practically all young composers
beyond the borders of national "schools,"
borders which had become questionable.
One can understand why, as a result of
such unity, a work was oftentimes ap-
plauded for its novelty rather than for
its purely musical value. Yet fashions

change while values remain constant and much of the music which enthralled audiences yesterday rightly has been forgotten so that wheat is separated from chaff. Furthermore, at all times a connection with the past must be re-established, and the new must find a bond with the old. Such is the innovation of tradition. These factors, then, characterize the music "Between the Wars" which in Germany, and only there, was called "New Music."

In the meantime the French had not resigned their tradition of moderateness and temperateness, qualities which conform to their general make-up, even though at first glance their music may have appeared wild and provocative. Even in such a work as Darius Milhaud's **Création du monde** there lives the spirit of Couperin. It is not just coincidence that the same Milhaud in his **Suite Pro-**

vençale utilizes themes of André Campra who hailed from Aix-en-Provence, as did Milhaud himself, and who in the early eighteenth century worked for the French court. Francis Poulenc, too, surrendered completely to French charm. He is scarcely touched by "New Music." Arthur Honegger, a German-Swiss belonging to **Les Six,** despite his many contacts with the French spirit embraced Max Reger and Richard Strauss much more thoroughly.

Italian music between the wars, represented by the names of Alfredo Casella and Francesco Malipiero, meant above all a renovation of tradition, that of the instrumental music of the **seicento** and the **settecento.** Paul Hindemith, finally, the **enfant terrible** of the twenties, became a masterly conserver of a specifically German tradition, combining as he did the craftsmanship of Johann Sebas-

18

tian Bach with the warmth in sonority and expression exuded by the post-romanticists.

In the realm of Eastern European music, Bela Bartok is easily the towering personality. In his youth he absorbed in a most individual manner the sonorous and harmonic innovations of French impressionism and of the Schoenberg before the conception of the "series." Subsequently, on the basis of his own scholarly analyses of Slavic and Arabian folk music he pushed forward into new realms. Finally, beginning with the Second Piano Concerto, he synthesized these innovations, excluding none of the musical elements, with the great tradition of nineteenth century Western Europe, a tradition which he had never abandoned, to be sure, even in his most audacious works. The quintessence of his creation, his string quartets are of an artistic value equalling those of Beethoven.

Both overt and hidden cross relations of "New Music" and romantic tradition can be found many times in the compositions of the following generation. In Germany, Wolfgang Fortner leads Hindemith's "concerted style" toward dodecaphonic music; Carl Orff most cleverly rejuvenates the cult theatre of primitive civilizations. In France, Olivier Messiaen, blending the coloristic splendor of romanticism with his own brand of rhythmic constructivism, couples an often sentimental primitiveness with orgiastic feats (which are hardly French). The combination may well be considered a reaction against the thesis of **goût** and **mesure** proclaimed in France in an all too doctrinaire manner. In Italy, Geoffredo Petrassi absorbs manifold inspirations that came to him from the West and

North without resigning, however, the classical approach renewed by Casella and Malipiero. Luigi Dallapiccola, on the other hand, finds a balance for the sensuous sounds of Italian opera in the dodecaphonic techniques of the Vienna school. These are just random examples characterizing the situation of European music before World War II.

The balance of innovation and tradition seemed accomplished. This fact, if so it be, is indicated also in various efforts undertaken in behalf of new interpretations of the old tonality which expanded its functions and dimensions. It is as though one wanted to insure its survival (see Hindemith's **The Craft of Musical Composition**). Schoenberg's revolutionary discovery of twelve-tone music was grasped by only a very small circle, mainly his personal disciples. Yet despite efforts to preserve tonality, confidence in it was definitely shaken. The theoretical compromises of the preceding generation, no less than their meager artistic results, had become an object of suspicion to the younger composers: **cui bono,** that neo-classical approach growing from romantic reminiscences, from historical consciousness and from progressive urges?

The situation demanded a definite solution, and a solution was found—to the great astonishment of the older generation—not by Schoenberg but by Anton von Webern. This Viennese composer, almost forgotten, who had lost his life after the end of World War II through a military accident, fast became the admired idol of the brightest among the young composers of Europe. From the terrifying experiences of a war which morally and materially had torn down all that had been considered solid, the young people escaped into the fascinating dreams of abstract, purely intellectual games. Webern was logical to the ultimate; together with tonality he had rid himself of all traditional forms. His a-formal and a-thematic music which allows but one order, that of the **Reihe,** exercised of necessity a magic power upon young people. It attracted all those seeking a way out of nihilist desperation. The grandiose technical inventions of our epoch opened new potentialities in sound for all of music, from the Trautonium via the Ondes Martenot to the electronic phenomena which youth slowly began to master. Under such circumstances, who would still be desirous of writing sonatas according to the well known recipes?

To the listeners the general confusion in music had become most puzzling even "Between the Wars." Those who had learned how to hammer out a four-hand piano arrangement of the **Eroica** would, of course, not know what to do with Hindemith. Those who, without pretense, played Haydn quartets in their homes were desperate, perhaps for sheer technical reasons, when confronted with Bartok's masterworks.

After World War I desperation engulfed also the experts. Amidst so many movements, one crossing the other, new ones and neo-old ones, they could not possibly know where to turn. Can one blame them? Nobody knows even today whither the road will take us. Perhaps to an anesthetizing magic of sound with novel instruments, perhaps to mathematical abstractions in sonority? Will it rebound to further artificially conjured up primitiveness, or to "neo-impressionist" nebulosities of tone figured out brilliantly on paper? Will it rebound to transcending lyrical stammering? Are we looking forward to a solid eclecticism which will adulterate everything produced by the music of the last hundred years? And what about the blue flower of romanticism? Does it not appear dried in the works of the young dodecaphonists, as if in an herbarium? Is it to come to life once more? Or are we perhaps heading toward a "new" cultural classicism in music, the possible result of a neo-cultural education? Can a truly new music grow at all from the vital feeling of our magnificent twentieth century? Or, after a hundred years of high flight, are we bound to disintegrate, to sink into complete insignificance? Is music to be but a stimulus for movie, television and sports? And: which of the two will be the victor, **museum** or **life?**

$\mathcal{I}$N THE MIDST OF A BABBLING of esthetic theories and doctrines, in the midst of confusion originated by creative energies on the one hand and every-day demands on the other, the work of Igor Stravinsky stands like a **rocher de bronze.**

To the development which we have attempted briefly to survey it has added decisive elements, particularly during the years "Between the Wars." Every composer, no matter how strong, at one time or the other has felt compelled to come to terms with Stravinsky, at least with his Russian period, and many have received abundant inspirations from his recent works. Nevertheless, it is also true that Stravinsky stands above the musical development of the first half of our century. He has constantly refused to wear himself out with problems only for the purpose of arriving at compromises and has solved problems with unique clairvoyance by employing strictly logical procedures.

For centuries European art had been torn between classicism and romanticism. The more dominating the manifestation of the artistic individual, the more violent was that struggle which, as we have seen, had culminated in the German music of the nineteenth century. This music signifies the victory of the individual over the omnivalidity of style, and at the same time the defeat of craftsmanship and of the craftsman's mentality by pathos or by "sensitive confessions." But the omni-validity of style and the mentality of the craftsman are the very things Stravinsky wishes to reconquer. This means a strict departure from romanticism, which we must fully understand in its entire concept.

Stravinsky as a musician of greatest alertness could not possibly fail to grasp the coloristic advances made by romantic music. He also has a real feeling for the sensuousness and melodic **élan.** In this respect we need only remember his admiration for Schubert, Weber and Tchaikovsky. However, with reference to Tchaikovsky in particular, Stravinsky's intellectuality becomes clear, an intellectuality completely divorcing him from romanticism, for he loves the Tchaikovsky of the small form, the Tchaikovsky of the elegant piano pieces, the

Tchaikovsky inspired by Mendelssohn's romantic classicism and by the French ballet. He loves Schubert—and Verdi, too—because of their spontaneous melodies. He loves Weber, "this prince of music," because of his knightly **grandezza.** In accordance with the famous Goethe word, he identifies classicism with health and romanticism with illness —of which he must necessarily be suspicious.

Stravinsky abhors that romanticism which has made music the mirror of emotional motives and hysteria. He cannot possibly sacrifice the speculative means of music to "that urge for expression," the word so often cited (and not by coincidence) in the musical esthetics of the German romantic period. "L'expression" —Stravinsky says in his **Chroniques de ma Vie**—"n'a jamais été la propriété immanente de la musique. La raison d'être

de celle-ci n'est d'aucune façon condition-
née par celle-là. Si, comme c'est presque
toujours le cas, la musique paraît ex-
primer quelque chose, ce n'est qu'une
illusion et non pas une réalité. C'est
simplement un élément additionnel que,
par une convention tacite et invétérée,
nous lui avons prêté, imposé, comme une
étiquette, un protocole, bref, une tenue
et que, par accoutumance ou inconsci-
ence, nous sommes arrivés à confondre
avec son essence."[1]

Romanticism had looked for an ever
richer ornamentation of this **tenue.** It
had created veritable **dresses de luxe**
overladen with pseudo-gold and luxuriat-
ing in a thousand colors when illuminated
by the projector's light of the stage or—
by the immoderate eyes of a modern
conductor.

We saw how musicians again and again
remembered (and always at the right

moment) the phenomenon of speculation which is the basis of their art, and how classical-constructivist tendencies were marshalled ever anew against the later romanticists' pulverization of sonority and color. In our epoch there is but one musician who with unerring eye recognized the borderlines between romanticism and classicism and who was able to draw the consequences from such recognition—Stravinsky. Himself a master of all combinations and devices in sonority, he has never allowed himself to be misled by them. He has utilized, and he has expanded, the arsenal of sound as a stylizing element in his early works, in which many to this day see the quintessence of his creativeness. It is exactly in such use that his **Petrouchka** is basically different from the **Salome** of Richard Strauss.

Stravinsky once said: "In the pure

state, music is free speculation." This sense for speculation had gradually diminished during the romantic era. Music had become a stimulant, and at times a drug. Stravinsky's music has nothing whatever to do with such a "drug"; instead, it is light, clear and translucent— even where it uses the gigantic apparatus of the modern orchestra, as in **Le Sacre du Printemps.** Stravinsky's music is cool, constructive and speculative, as is the music of Joseph Haydn whom he admires so much. Is it, for that reason, a music without a soul? Of course not! And yet so often exactly that has been argued. Only if one synonymizes soul with pathos and emotional exhibitionism could such a verdict stand.

However, synonymization of that kind had been the prerogative of the romantic school from Berlioz to Wagner. All other epochs subordinated emotional motives to an intellectual order which organized and (by means of such organization) humanized them—from Dufay to Beethoven, from Monteverdi to Brahms. The emotional motives nurture fantasy, they help shape imagination. Every human being, no matter how far removed from genius, has hundreds of ideas every day. Often they do not even penetrate consciousness. Without such ideas or imagination there can be no creative activity. On the other hand, imagination does not make an "art work." One surely must not under-estimate it, but one should by no means over-appraise it, as Hans Pfitzner did in his rather naive theory.

"Invention presupposes imagination but should not be confused with it," we read in Stravinsky's **Poetics of Music** (Poétique Musicale, Paris, 1946. Translated as Poetics of Music, Cambridge, Mass., 1947), "for the act of invention

33

implies the necessity of a lucky find and of achieving full realization of this find. What we imagine does not necessarily take on a concrete form and may remain in a state of virtuality, whereas invention is not conceivable apart from its actually being worked out.

"Thus, what concerns us here is not imagination in itself, but rather creative imagination: the faculty that helps us to pass from the level of conception to the level of realization."

In the art work, this realization is what matters; it is the result of much effort and it takes time. Beethoven's sketchbooks speak an eloquent language. What, then, is the task of the composer? To make a careful survey and appraisal of his ideas and his imagination, to select his ideas and "organize" them. Stravinsky, in his writings, again and again returns to the concept of order. To that concept all his efforts and all his projects are devoted. This fact fully corresponds to the craftsman's approach to art.

"Art in the true sense is a way of fashioning works according to certain methods acquired either by apprenticeship or by inventiveness," writes Stravinsky. And another time he says: "Composing, for me, is putting into an order a certain number of these sounds according to certain interval relationships." These words may sound like a degradation of artistic creativity—they definitely will to those who believe the activity of the artist to be a sort of trance situation which overcomes him in the so-called "blessed moments." Trance, however, does not last long. Scores created in such situations can scarcely be more than miserable ink spots.

Stravinsky would be the last to deny the frequently cited inspiration. "I have no thought of denying to inspiration the outstanding role that has devolved upon it in the generative process we are studying; I simply maintain that inspiration is in no way a prescribed condition of the creative act, but rather a manifestation that is chronologically secondary." In inspiration he sees "une force motrice qu'on trouve dans n'importe quelle activité humaine et **qui n'est nullement le monopole des artistes.** Mais cette force ne se déploie que quand elle est mise en action par un effort, et cet effort est le travail."[2]

Such a concept of artistic activity is in diametric contrast to the separation of form and content as maintained by the musical esthetics of the romantic movement. Everything creative was included by the representatives of such esthetics in the nebulous idea of "content." Form to them was but a necessary evil, a kind of undignified writing act which the composer exercised according to paper rules. What degradation of art is exhibited in such an approach! According to that concept, the great masters of the Middle Ages who always used the same themes and therefore represented always identical "content" were simply craftsmen—the word used in a modern, contemptuous manner. However, in reality, craft means a most honorable and proud thing: ability developed to mastery. Modern thinkers like Montaigne speak correctly of "painters, poets and other **craftsmen,**" a matter emphasized in Stravinsky's **Poetics.** Artists of great ability such as Hindemith attribute, and not in vain, deep significance to craftsmanship.

Those who recognize the factor of "organizing activity" of the creative human being cannot possibly regard form as but an empty scheme, a barren skeleton which must be filled with content. Rather they will look upon it as the proper and true manifestation of productive energy. With the organizing thought of the composer, his inspiration and imagination gain that concreteness, plasticity and intensity which alone lend validity to his art work. In this organization his very artistry is contained, and it must prove and manifest itself ever anew in every one of his projects and tasks—the word Stravinsky likes so much.

Through the unique power of organization the true creator can be distinguished from the academic **routinier.** And yet—has not Stravinsky more frequently than any one else been accused of "academicism?" Yes—and such accusations, as a rule, come from a confusion of ideas caused by the musical esthetics of the romanticists and evident in many modern writings on music.

The writers were so thoroughly embarrassed by their predecessors' unresponsive attitude to the new in the course of the last hundred years that now they were suddenly swept by a real "mania for progress." They became suspicious of all relations to tradition, so that everything that sounded new was, if not a revelation, at least a road toward the future. Thus they frequently confused appearance with substance, the dress with that which it was to cover. What a wonderful chance for charlatans!

Stravinsky, in reality, is the very opposite to the academician, a personality of such immediacy and spontaneity of expression in the most important as well as the least important things of life that he is almost incomparable. He brooks no half-way measures. He never stands on the sidelines. Everything commands his undivided attention. Every one of his

reactions betrays the "total individual."
"I do not have a temperament suited to
academicism; so I always use academic
formulas knowingly as I would use folklore. They are raw materials of my
work."

This utilization of "raw materials" has
produced much misunderstanding of
Stravinsky, and this misunderstanding
is the result of insufficient familiarity
with Stravinsky's artistic thought. We
saw that he regards organization and
construction as manifestations of artistic
creativeness. Naturally he is not indifferent to the substance of sound, to sonority, any more than painters or sculp-
tors of former epochs were indifferent to
the selection of their theme from the total
treasury of subject matter laid down by
convention. However, theme, sonority
and substance to Stravinsky are only
ways of obtaining meaning for the art

work — and that through organization. Did not Bach and Handel base some of their most significant works on the thematic ideas of others? They, too, saw the activity of composing mainly in organization and in construction, as did the artists of the entire Western civilization prior to the French Revolution.

Stravinsky stands solidly in our time. "Cultural escapism" which seeks refuge in the supposedly better past is far from his horizon. He hates the snobbish estheticism of the "cultural pessimists." On the other hand, as an individual of our time, he cannot divest himself of the culture and education which determine our intellectual existence to a much greater degree than would be admitted by most Europeans today.

Historical perspective is an approach deeply influencing all Western thinking. There is scarcely an intellectual response in us which could be called devoid of historical consciousness. Our knowledge and our absorption of culture is, in fact, so general that, for instance, a modern human being simply cannot pass by Romanesque or Gothic art works, as Goethe was still able to do, without paying attention to their subtle differences. Today we can no longer hear music without, perhaps unconsciously, surrendering to historical comparisons. Only through such historical attitudes have Bach, Mozart and Beethoven become living ideas. Whenever "actual experiences" have failed us in our attempt to come to terms with the present, historic knowledge has caused us to escape into the past, has led us to a "museum attitude" and to excessive worship of the cultural achievements of earlier periods. Thus a large contingent of European music lovers is satisfied with "museum worship." Their ears are more or less deaf to the voices of the present.

A powerful expansion of our historical consciousness has taken place, even more so since the cultures of remote countries have invaded our minds. What would modern art be without our understanding of the exotic peoples, or of past civilizations gone since millenia? What would modern music be had we no knowledge of the vast treasures of the past redeemed from oblivion by musicological research during the last hundred years? Without archaeology how would Thomas Mann have written his "Joseph" cycle?

The Russian Stravinsky grew into Western historicity with that logic that is part of his individuality. Once he had absorbed Russian folklore he entered, with **L'Histoire du Soldat, Mavra** and **Pulcinella,** the realm of European experiences, and with almost every work he expanded his own perspective of history. A product of the classic-Italian tradition of Russian music, he felt attracted more powerfully to the Latin cycle than to the Germanic—for the latter had been encumbered by the mystical dusk of romanticism ever since Wolfram von Eschenbach. To a creator of Stravinsky's spontaneity it would be unthinkable to utilize historical elements with scientific exactitude, with "work fidelity." He is interested in a creative transformation and complete repossession. He is an **homme de proie,** as C. F. Ramuz correctly states.

To speak further in the manner of Ramuz, Stravinsky is both primitive and sophisticated, or, to put it differently: in one person he is the elemental Russian and the highly cultivated European of recent vintage. Having heard Stravinsky conduct his own works only once, one knows how even the most charming of his compositions suddenly assumes awesome, elemental aspects. The primitiveness of his personality pushes through again and again (and unexpectedly so), but it is always controlled by an inexorably severe thought of order, the common denominator of all his works.

Stravinsky, then, uses the past as material—not exactly respectfully, but with the proud egoism of an autonomous artist. He is not averse to going back within one work to Handel and to Verdi, or to Vivaldi and, at the same time, to jazz. As a creative engineer he acts with complete sovereignty and, seeing in the act of organizing the very function of the composer, he permits himself complete generosity with respect to musical building materials. The objections so frequently propounded against him, which culminate in the baseless contention that he adorns himself with the feathers of others, are thus answered.

As long as he utilized only Russian folklore, Stravinsky, strangely enough, never was reproached, because the "connoisseurs" for decades had been accustomed to the fact that Russian composers like to embellish the substance of their country's folk music with modern sonorities. Writers docile and humble in regard to Stravinsky's "Russian" works were thoroughly startled, however, when Stravinsky began to utilize idioms of European music. We remember that one of the best known German music critics of the twenties, for instance, called Stravinsky "the chameleon of modern music," contending that the composer would show a new face in every work, perhaps just for the purpose of making fools of his listeners. Honor to his ashes — one

46

could scarcely misunderstand Stravinsky's Western message more thoroughly!

But let us try to understand. Was it not necessarily confusing to musical observers-at-large—observers who had long been accustomed to composers repeating their style once fixed—when Stravinsky with every new work confronted them with a need for a new and a final solution of a certain problem? Stravinsky called it "the task which I set myself." He solves each task once and forever and never, or rarely, returns to it. If he does, as in the two late symphonies, it really concerns two completely different types.

Stravinsky had recognized with penetrating logic from the very outset that the "late" and overripe situation of European music suggested but two possibilities. One was continuing on the pathway of the romanticists—as Schoenberg and his disciples were doing, and as the neo-

Webernists, among the younger, are doing today—and the other was a return
to the classical approach, the approach
he chose. It took a Stravinsky, to be sure,
to make such a decision without stagnat-
ing in classicism, which means in historical consciousness and in a resulting imitation of classical prototypes.

He intentionally ignored a number of
discoveries of modern music in order to
find his way back to the true tradition
of Western music and to renew it with
the vital feeling of our time. He is one
of the few masters of the twentieth century who obtains that "higher order" of
the old masters about which we spoke
before. And just as the old masters, he,
too, subjects his strong individuality to a
severe compulsion—willingly and intentionally. He rejects the freedom whose
perils he knows all too well, that un-
limited freedom of artistic utterance

which had alienated music from the public in the most terrifying manner, so much so that the most recent attempts of composers address themselves to the smallest circle of specialists and can be heard only in the broadcasting studios during late-night shows.

Stravinsky adheres to a law which he formulates for himself and the limitations of which he keeps increasingly narrow. It is certainly not just coincidence that ancient subjects play such a great role in his work. He sees in them the perfect creations of Humanism, that Humanism toward which he himself tends with ever-intensified awareness. He does not wish to give us modern interpretations of the legends of Oedipus, Apollo, Persephone and Orpheus. He wants to re-awaken their spirit with his modern musical language. His music in the truest sense of the word is humane, and for that reason it radiates that characteristic which had been lost in all modern music: **serenitas.**

This humaneness of Stravinsky's music accomplishes its stylistic unity. We know that in speaking of stylistic unity with regard to Stravinsky's work many connoisseurs who have followed us to this point—perhaps hesitatingly—will skeptically shake their heads. We can hear them whisper: "This is going too far! Unity of style in, of all composers, Stravinsky!?" "Does his music not scintillate in a thousand colors like a kaleidoscope?" we hear them ask. "Does he not mix the most heterogeneous elements of style without hesitation?" This all may be true, is our answer; however, it in no way alters the fact that Stravinsky makes all the building stones, large or small, of the past which he has chosen for his own use, his own, and completely so. He melts them in the fire of his organizing constructivism.

The romantic experience has often misled us into confusing style with personal signature. The general idea of style has thus been narrowed down to the style of one person. However, a composer who wants to achieve omnivalidity cannot possibly be satisfied with his personal style alone. He must go beyond that, just as Mozart did, especially in his operas, in which he amalgamated all essential stylistic elements of the eighteenth century and in so doing did not shy away from historical reminiscences which were part of the cultural awareness of his time. Stravinsky, utilizing all the experiences which offer themselves, does not care about the manifestation of his personality, but he is emphatic on the manifestation of an artistic concept as mirrored in his personality. We see the stylistic

51

unity of Stravinsky's **oeuvre** in his mentality. It is the identity of this artistic spirit which joins **Petrouchka** with **Persephone, Le Sacre du Printemps** with **Orpheus, Les Noces** with **Oedipus Rex.** And that spirit is the spirit of **classicism in art.**

*I*GOR FEDOROVICH STRAVINS-
ky was born on June 17, 1882, in Oranienbaum, near St. Petersburg, the summer
residence of his father. He hails from the
conservative world of Russian aristoc-
racy. His father Feodor was one of the
most celebrated opera singers of his time,
a well-to-do man of fine reputation who
raised his children in strict family traditions and in the no less strict Greek
Orthodox faith. Strictness has left deep
traces in Stravinsky's personality.

In accordance with the autocracy in old Russian tradition no son is permitted to choose his profession himself. Igor was expected to take up law and he studied jurisprudence at the St. Petersburg University and took the graduating examinations there. The profession of Stravinsky's father allowed the son, however, to become familiar with music from his earliest childhood. The music of Mikhail Glinka was the guiding star of his youth. Piano lessons, customary for sons of well-to-do parents, while affording him little pleasure were decisive for his attitude toward the phenomenon of sound.

He grew up with sonorities before becoming engaged in compositional exercises which, based on old-fashioned rules, were never to his liking. He much preferred spending his time in the circles of progressive painters and literati. Through these he met the vanguard of art, and particularly of French art.

During a vacation spent with his parents in Germany he met Rimsky-Korsakoff in Heidelberg. Among the Russian composers of that era Rimsky was doubtless the artist with the best schooling and who as a teacher enjoyed absolute authority. Stravinsky was thoroughly disappointed when the famed master showed so little enthusiasm for his first compositional attempts. He was not completely turned down, however, and Rimsky recommended that Stravinsky engage in more thorough studies of compositional technique. Recognizing the originality of the young man's artistic makeup, he dissuaded him from attending the St. Petersburg Conservatory ("que l'atmosphère de cette institution n'était pas faite pour moi") and suggested private lessons with one of his students.

After the death of his father Stravinsky came into even closer contact with Rimsky. He studied form, analysis and particularly instrumentation with him. His assignments consisted of orchestrations of piano works by Beethoven and Schubert. Stravinsky was completely aware of being trained in old-fashioned concepts for meanwhile he had encountered new perspectives through a man who was to become very significant for Stravinsky's future. And these fresh ideas had blown into the Russian capital on winds from the West.

The man in question was Sergei Diaghilev, founder of the Russian Ballet. When Stravinsky met this ingenious inspirer of modern art, Diaghilev was the editor of a vanguard art magazine as well as the impresario of modern art exhibits. Only later did he found the famed ballet ensemble whose much admired stars were Pavlova, Karsavina and Nijinsky. Through the stimulating circle of Sergei Diaghilev, Stravinsky became acquainted with the music of Claude Debussy.

This is scarcely the place to describe Debussy's significance for modern music, but it should be remarked that it was Debussy who once and for all pushed through the limitations of functional-tonal thinking and who invented a new method for both the construction and the juxtaposition of chords. He contrasted the dynamic principle of the leading tone (which had led from Wagner's **Tristan** to Schoenberg with undiminished vigor) with the static principle, that of a free succession of multi-functional sounds all based upon seventh chords. He gave this principle reality in a new compositional technique which supersedes the thematic-symphonic workmanship that had been applied for a full century, replacing it with a succession of harmonic complexes of manifold tonal derivations. At the same time, he invented a light, transparent and more tentative type of instrumentation in which coloristic nuances were no longer blended but rather juxtaposed with the most delicate sensitivity. These innovations left their marks in the early works of Igor Stravinsky.

Of such traces we notice little in his first major composition, the **Symphony in E flat major,** opus 1, dedicated to his teacher Rimsky. It is a pupil's work following the symphonies of Alexander Glazounov with regard to structure and, in substance, the standard works of that epoch. However, one thing is undeniable: even here we find complete mastery of orchestral treatment. Naturally, this mastery is based upon experiences gathered from Rimsky-Korsakoff, but the orchestration has freshness and, particularly in the **scherzo,** a lustre which allows us to anticipate the young master of **L'Oiseau de Feu.**

This mastery is advanced to virtuosity in the two following orchestral works of the young composer: the **Scherzo Fantastique** and the **Feu d'artifice.** As indicated in the titles, we here deal with compositions of the much admired realm of French impressionism. The **Scherzo** was inspired by Maeterlinck's famed **Vie des abeilles. Feu d'artifice,** thematically speaking, derives from Debussy himself. Despite that "painting in sound" the two scores are clearly distinguishable from the impressions of French artists—they are of a logic in thematic construction and, above all, of a plasticity in sonority which seems concrete, almost bodily alive. When Diaghilev heard these works during the winter of 1909 in a concert of modern compositions conducted by Siloti in St. Petersburg, he at once intuitively recognized that Stravinsky was the man to compose a ballet which he had planned for his troupe for the following season. The resulting work originated Stravinsky's world-wide reputation which to this day rests on **L'Oiseau de Feu.**

This score, too, has all the earmarks of a work of youth; but it is the early work of a master who is on his way—to himself. The choreography and story by Fokine, based on a Russian legend, describes the struggle of the Firebird, the spirit of good, with the magician Kastchei, the spirit of evil. Of course, it ends with the defeat of Kastchei in the triumphal manner that can be expected in a Russian "pomp" opera.

The Infernal Dance of Kastchei and his followers is the most original and the most significant part of the ballet. In the representation of demoniacal powers the elemental temperament of our composer manifests itself for the first time. And what an abundance of bizarre sonorities, of terrifying accents, and of rhythms arbitrarily disobeying the meter! The sound picture is delineated by the most penetrating instruments of the orchestra, trumpets, trombones, xylophone and piano, which are given solo billing in a manner characteristic of Stravinsky. The complexity of sound phenomena, however, does not prevent a most solid and logical construction. The "Danse Infernale," a good example of the "almost graspable plasticity" of Stravinsky's music, of which we previously spoke, is most original. In Western music theretofore unknown, it testifies to the composer's power to translate the gestures of dancing into musical forms.

Stravinsky's music has an incomparable "gestic" concreteness. It delineates pantomime and motion unmistakably and clearly. Owing to this faculty Stravinsky could emerge as the greatest ballet creator of music. We intentionally say "ballet creator," for through him ballet has become an autonomous musical form. In former times one wrote music, occasionally very good music, which could be danced. Stravinsky esteems such music highly, as may be seen from the fact that in his later works he likes to utilize it, and indeed in **L'Oiseau de Feu** "classical" reminiscences are suggested. Stravinsky, however, does not write music which **can** be danced, as a rule, but music which **must** be danced. It is the mirror, in sound, of the essence of dance, gesture in panto-mime.

In comparison with the "Danse Infer-nale" the other parts of **L'Oiseau de Feu** amount to little. All are brilliantly or-chestrated, to be sure, as, for instance, the Firebird Variations—from the point of view of pantomime fascinating indeed —or the pompous but not happily de-veloped Finale. They indicate that Stra-vinsky had learned a great deal from a master like Rimsky-Korsakoff, and also that he knew how to develop in an inde-pendent, progressive manner what he had absorbed.

Diaghilev's commission for this famed ballet had come from Paris by telegram. In reactionary St. Petersburg there was a powerful opposition to Diaghilev, so strong that the propagator of modern Russian art, particularly since the unrest of 1905, preferred living in the free air of the French capital, then at the zenith of its "liberal splendor." With art exhibitions and opera performances Diaghilev had introduced himself in the best way possible, but the great sensation was to be the guest performances of his Russian Ballet.

Today no one can possibly imagine the effect of that splendor of colors, artistic luxury and virtuosity of dancing in which these performances excelled. Like an elemental tornado from "un-drained" Asia, these ballets whirled over the Parisian stages. Everyone seemed mesmerized by these Eastern revelations. Only those familiar with the dusty mannerisms and the unbelievable lack of musicality in Parisian opera ballets can imagine the sensation these highly cultivated Russians produced.

This was unheard-of luck for Stravinsky—his Parisian debut coinciding with the Parisians' glowing enthusiasm for the Russians. The unknown composer from Oranienbaum became the celebrated hero of the day with one stroke. The première of **L'Oiseau de Feu** took place on June 25, 1910 in the Paris Opera with Karsavina in the title role and Gabriel Pierné conducting.

After this first brilliant encounter with Paris, Stravinsky felt deeply attracted by France. In France the musicians whom he had admired most from afar and whose works had impressed him so much lived and worked: Dukas, Falla, Ravel and, above all, Debussy. Literary Paris, too, exercised a tremendous fascination on the master who preferred the acquaintance of painters and writers to that of professional musicians. France became Stravinsky's second home. In France the Russian developed into a citizen of the world. France led him to his classical approach in the arts. In 1934, France made him a **citoyen** of the much maligned and yet so impressive **Troisième République.**

For the time being, Stravinsky was the musical exponent of that ravishing Russian art for which the hearts of France were frantically beating. Even while working on **L'Oiseau de Feu** Stravinsky was projecting a new ballet the theme of which was to be the celebration of spring in pagan Russia, the Russia of primeval times. The project was shelved for a while when a new idea entered his mind. He was at that time with his family —in 1906 he had married his cousin, Catherine Nossenko—in Clarens at Lake Geneva which in the difficult years of World War I became his idyllic refuge.

"Avant d'aborder le **Sacre du Printemps,** dont la réalisation se présentait longue et laborieuse, je voulus me divertir à une oeuvre orchestrale où le piano jouait un rôle prépondérant, une sorte de **Konzertstueck.** En composant cette musique, j'avais nettement la vision d'un pantin subitement déchaîné qui, par ses cascades d'arpèges diaboliques, exaspère la patience de l'orchestre, lequel, à son tour, lui réplique par des fanfares menaçantes. Ce morceau bizarre achevé, je cherchai pendant des heures, en me promenant au bord du Léman, le titre qui exprimerait en un seul mot le caractère de ma musique et, conséquemment, la figure de mon personnage. Un jour, je sursautai de joie.

"Pétrouchka! l'éternel et malheureux héros de toutes les foires, de tous les pays!"[3]

Thus Stravinsky describes the creation

of the work which laid the foundation for his world-wide reputation as the master of modern music. The mentioned **Konzertstueck** became the second **tableau** in the new "choreographic drama" which he worked out with the famous painter Alexandre Benois who designed the scenery and costumes. An additional movement was already completed, a Russian Dance, which now has its place at the end of the first **tableau.** The idea of using the puppet tragedy of Petrouchka within the framework of the old St. Petersburg Carnival is Diaghilev's. He and Benois would have been bad entrepeneurs had their new work failed to take advantage of the Paris enthusiasm for Russian folklore. And had not Stravinsky indicated this direction himself when associating the first movement of his **Konzertstueck** with Petrouchka, that poor puppet perishing through love for the capricious ballerina, a love brutally destroyed by the Moor?

Of course, he uses melodic elements of national Russian origin. He not only dresses them in the modern timbre of the orchestra as his predecessors had done (and as he himself had done in certain parts of **L'Oiseau de Feu),** but he transforms them by means of his fantasy into grotesque entities, flashes of lightning, furious and melancholy gestures expressed through sound. And how novel the treatment of the piano is with its violent chains of chords, tonally fixed, to be sure, yet harmonically no longer "functional!" The winds, in accordance with their specific character, acquire hitherto unknown independence. In the **Konzertstueck** the tritone (which already had played an important role in **L'Oiseau de Feu)** is elevated to a harmonic "leading motive," in that Stravinsky sounds simultaneously C major and F sharp major in the famous fanfare.

The center of the second **tableau** is the dance of the coquettish ballerina accompanying herself on the **cornet à piston.** For the first time we become aware of Stravinsky's love for the waltz. It is a frequent mistake to consider this dance a parody. With reference to later works, such as the **Suites for Small Orchestra** and even **L'Histoire du Soldat,** critics have used the word "parody" indiscriminately. Due to the excesses of pathos in the music of the post-romanticists they had lost the understanding for **esprit** and capricious humor. In a witty and clever way Stravinsky cleanses the waltz of all the **schmalz** with which it had been surfeited by sentimental café-house musicians. A few, pungent instruments led by the **cornet à piston** do the job, plus an ostinato rhythm mixed with 2/4 meter—

disobeying all rules and traditions. The Viennese waltz has been reduced to its naked sound substance.

The element of rhythm, so long neglected in all European music, appears in **Petrouchka** with uncommon severity, with special importance attached to the odd rhythmic beats, rather than to the even. Small intervals are repeated with upsetting obstinacy. The technique of the ostinato is foreshadowed, a technique later to become one of the most significant means of Stravinsky's musical constructions. Much of this music is inspired by visual impressions and associations, and at the same time worked out with precision, clarity and with the logic of form, so that the result is not identical with the art works of musical impressionism. Most personal is Stravinsky's method of concretizing even those ideas which he had received undeniably from

French impressionism. This is seen in the much admired **tour de passe** in the first **tableau.** The folklore parts are the most conventional stretches of this work. But even for them he has such magnificent ideas as the scare chords of the trombones and tuba in the Coach Dance of the last **tableau.** The finale of the ballet, in which the ghostlike figure of the dead Petrouchka appears on the puppet stage, is one of a magical transcendence which Stravinsky achieves again only once more, in the last picture of his recent **The Rake's Progress.**

Petrouchka was produced by Diahilev's Ballets Russes at the Théâtre du Châtelet in Paris on June 13, 1911. Michel Fokine was the choreographer, Nijinsky danced the title role, and Pierre Monteux conducted.

Petrouchka pushed Igor Stravinsky into the front line of the musical vanguard. His next ballet, **Le Sacre du Printemps,** made him an admired revolutionary in the eyes of his contemporaries, and the object of endless ovations. Finally the scandal came without which public opinion does not bestow such a title upon anyone: the first performance of **Le Sacre** in Paris at the Théâtre des Champs Elysées on May 29, 1913. Nijinsky was both choreographer and star and again Monteux conducted.

This really was "new music." Outbursts of rhythm's elemental powers, a sizzling, shocking, pounding, seemingly without order, propelling and overwhelming — thus **Le Sacre du Printemps** appeared to the listeners of 1913. They overlooked that the scandal was caused only to a small degree by the music, that it was largely the result of an inadequate and unmusical choreography by Nijinsky. A stylization of old oriental models was the craze and he had tried to apply such stylization of gesture and pantomime to, of all things, these "Tableaux of Pagan Russia." Diaghilev had used a representative of the Dalcroze School of Geneva as his assistant, and she had counseled Nijinsky on rhythmic gymnastics. It is clear that this kind of pedagogical approach to the dance was not applicable to the highly complicated musical events of **Le Sacre du Printemps;** the result was choreographic chaos.

The "shocking" effect of the music of **Le Sacre** rests on its displacement of the values of the basic musical elements: melody, harmony and rhythm. Melody had dominated in classical music. In the romantic movement, harmony increasingly had gained independence and power until in many works of the later nineteenth century rhythm had completely disintegrated under harmony's tyrannic rule, a rule which had subordinated even melody. The main accent in **Le Sacre du Printemps** is on rhythm. As an element it subordinates harmony which, in turn, frequently is but a means of intensifying rhythmic events, and it equally subordinates melody for long stretches by contracting it to small and constantly repeated motives. The harmony, on the other hand, rests on bitonality, already applied in the preceding ballets, but now elevated to a principle and enriched by alterations of the fundamental chord. The melodic building stones of the score are condensations of Russian folk music and are, accordingly, strongly diatonic.

While Stravinsky in **L'Oiseau de Feu** and in **Petrouchka** borrows entire complexes of melody from Russian folk music, in **Le Sacre** a constructive manner transforms the material borrowed from foreign realms and condenses and epitomizes it. **Le Sacre,** from all we know, has but one original melody, the feared bassoon solo at the beginning.

It is a mistake, however, to regard **Le Sacre du Printemps** as only an expression of rhythmic elemental powers, as was done for a long time. Instead, there are two basic characteristics inherent in the work. One is pronouncedly delicate and sensitive, and is most clearly evident in the introductions to both parts, unthinkable without the influences of Debussy and Ravel (even though Stravinsky has transformed these influences into a hard, cool language). The other characteristic is the elemental rhythm of which we spoke and which, particularly toward the end of the two tableaux, breaks through with incredible harshness. For long passages the orchestra, consisting of more than a hundred men, becomes a tremendous percussive instrument.

The essence of the rhythmic events lies in the absence of symmetry. During several centuries our music had been organized in a symmetrical manner, a manner conspicuous in every classical melody. The exciting and at the same time shocking effect of **Le Sacre** is derived from the fact that no symmetrical succession of rhythms obtains. The rhythms constantly change with every measure even when the meter remains identical. And these rhythms with many ingenious changes run against the so-called "strong" beats of the measure. However, in the final scenes, meter itself changes with every bar.

It has frequently been contended that **Le Sacre du Printemps** started the invasion of uncivilized Asia and her elemental vigor into European music. One can scarcely sustain such an opinion. The score is created with a **raffinement,** with a cleverness that testifies much more to the over-civilized atmosphere of 1913 than to primitive culture. How absurd to assume that Stravinsky is a "primitive Russian!" He himself would strongly repudiate such a term. His concern for rhythmic problems has nothing whatever to do with primitiveness. Instead, the reason for such concern was the literary subject matter of the ballet—aside from a certain historical outlook previously discussed. We are here confronted with scenes from the pagan world of ancient Russia; and that world had to be given shape through music. Stravinsky saw in rhythm the ideal element for his realization of such a task. Nor can we underestimate the illustrative components of **Le Sacre** as we admire the "absolute" musical solution found by the composer. **Le Sacre du Printemps** is based upon visual and literary associations, too, and as a conception it corresponds to the most fundamental desire for a modern style.

Stravinsky has vigorously protested against the label "revolutionary" just because he wrote **Le Sacre du Printemps. Le Sacre** to him was a special "case," which posed certain musical, and technical, problems. These problems had to be and were solved. As always, he then turned to an entirely new task. Even today there are people who complain woefully that Stravinsky abandoned the road of steady revolutionary progress (the road on which **Le Sacre du Printemps** was a flamboyant marker) and that the master gradually turned into an academician. They misunderstand the essence of Stravinsky's personality. Notwithstanding all incontestable innovations brought about by **Le Sacre,** the work still marks the end of Stravinsky's youthful period, one of learning and of gathering experiences. With that work Stravinsky had investigated all the tools, as it were; from now on he is less and less interested in subject matter and themes. He is not emphatic on what prompts his music. All his work, all his thinking and searching now centers on the autonomy of sonority; and even if his sounds are arrived at in closest connection with a text or with a choreography, yet it is always the autonomy of sound which holds Stravinsky's attention.

Departure from stylization of choreographic situations by means of a "gestic" type of music and the resulting turn to absoluteness of musical construction is achieved in Stravinsky's next great work, **Les Noces,** the result of a nine-year-long effort which repeatedly had been interrupted by other projects and assignments. Financially these years were the most difficult for our young composer. World War I had broken out. The contact with Russia upon which Stravinsky depended with tender affection had been cut off. More than anything else, this affection for his native country, which he has never seen again, determined his adherence to Russian themes. To be sure, he found solutions that had nothing whatever to do with the "choreographic dramas" of his youth.

The decisive features in this new development are resignation of color and bril-

liance and, together with them, abandonment of the large orchestra as used in the
post-romantic era, radical reduction of
sonorities, incorporation of song beyond
any lyric-dramatic formulae heretofore
valid, and the plastic shaping of melody.
All these features indicate tendencies toward a classical approach, an attitude as-
sumed by a man who had recognized and
discovered himself. What marvelous solutions were found in those decisive years
spent chiefly at Lake Geneva in friendly
association with two remarkable person-
alities to whom Stravinsky is indebted
for many an inspiration: the Swiss poet
C. F. Ramuz, whose **Souvenirs sur Igor
Stravinsky** admirably captures the personality of the composer, and the conductor Ernest Ansermet, who had conducted the American première of **L'Oiseau de Feu** in 1916. Now we must entirely separate the stage works from in-

strumental music. His interest in the latter is increased for herein he sees the purest embodiment of the principle of "autonomous" creation.

In the realm of the stage Stravinsky invents a type one could perhaps call narrative musical theatre. All events are stylized in strict musical forms, chained to each other, as it were, like architectural links. The result means elimination of all dramatic, emotional moments on which the "ups and downs" of the music drama depended. **Les Noces** is called "Russian Dance Scenes with Music and Song," but the music actually achieves a degree of immobility which hardly can be transformed into dancing.

We have certain photographs, from the period of Stravinsky's activities at Lake Geneva taken during World War I, which show the composer seated at the piano surrounded by numerous drums of various sizes, triangles and other percussion instruments. This is the orchestra of the four scenes of the "Russian Peasant Wedding," partly melancholy, partly exuberant and even grotesque. In the orchestra —its make-up became a matter of experimentation for several years to come—we find, aside from the four pianos, only percussion instruments. Rhythm therefore determines the sound picture even more decisively, if that is possible, than it had done in **Le Sacre.** It is also considerably simplified. The character of the score lies in its machine-like inexorability. There is no room whatever for the chanted lyricism Stravinsky still used in the impressionistically encumbered opera **Rossignol,** the creation of which reaches from early Russian years to World War I, and which found its definitive form in the symphonic poem **Le Chant du Rossignol.**

Stravinsky at this time was much con-

cerned with Russian folk poetry. "Ce qui
me séduisait dans ces vers, ce n'est pas
autant les anecdotes, souvent truculentes,
ni les images ou les métaphores toujours
délicieusement imprévues, que l'enchaî-
nement des mots et des syllabes, ainsi que
la cadence qu'il provoque et qui produit
sur notre sensibilité un effet tout proche
de celui de la musique." [4]

These sentences from **Chroniques de
ma Vie** (Paris, 1935) characterize the
vocal characteristics of **Les Noces.** Stravinsky constructs tiny thematic building
stones from folklore elements, and he re-
peats them with greatest alertness in constantly altered scansion so that he can
play one thematic fragment out against
another. Sliding, cackling, whining **ap-
poggiature** heighten the affective content.
Thus a score, at the same time rigid and
unbelievably vital, originates. There is
no choice, in a scenic presentation, other

than to separate dancing and singing—
so great are the musical difficulties. The
dancers act, and the choristers sing in the
orchestra.

The separation of pantomime and song
discloses new possibilities for the narrative musical theatre. In his next work
Stravinsky makes these potentials a dramatic principle: the animal burlesque
Renard is based essentially on an original
Russian folk tale, the tale of the rooster,
cat and goat which at the end capture the
rapacious fox and kill it. Ramuz with
painstaking effort had translated the Russian text into French, word by word. The
animals are represented by clowns: two

tenors and two basses seated in the orchestra sing the text. Stylistically **Renard** lies in the neighborhood of **Les Noces,** yet in lieu of hard vocal scansion here there is hilarious life ranging from snarling, sneering chatter to grotesquely caricaturing tirades. Despite the strong characterization (which just as in **Les Noces** is not based upon vocal "interpretation" of words, but lies rather in the musical substance of the singing parts, and which is made even more emphatic through solo effects of the orchestra) **Renard** fails to produce the immediate effect emanating from **Les Noces.** The vocal principle is overdone as a result of the grotesqueness that prompts it, and the orchestral realization is too incoherent and restless. **Renard** is an experiment also in that Stravinsky uses a cymbal, impressed by the artistry of Aladar Racz—and it will always be difficult to find a good player for that instrument. (Recently Stravinsky has substituted a piano for the cymbal.)

The year 1918 was particularly hard for Stravinsky, for through the treaty of Brest-Litovsk he was cut off from his homeland and his income. As his financial situation became critical he hit upon a strange self-help project together with his friend Ramuz. They decided to write a dramatic play for a very small ensemble with which they would go on tour, in the manner of traveling comedy troupes, from one Swiss city to another. Ramuz wrote a libretto based on the old Russian folk legend of the soldier who sells his soul to the devil. Through the love of a princess who recovers from a fatal illness through the magic of his violin playing, he is freed from the devil, yet he succumbs at the end. Not content with his new happiness, he wants to see his home and his old mother again. On the way he must pass the border, and there the devil seizes him. This is a Faustian subject with surprising similarity to Stravinsky's more recent **The Rake's Progress.** The painter René Auberjaunois created the most primitive **décors,** Stravinsky wrote the score and Ansermet conducted. There was just one performance, however; the Spanish influenza became epidemic in Switzerland and the dream of new riches had to be quickly buried.

That is the story of the origin of the now world-famous **L'Histoire du Soldat.** It says on the score, "to be read, played and danced." Narrative musical theatre that had been the goal of **Renard** was a reality for the first time. It is the narrator who reports the action. Three persons demonstrate it in a sort of pantomimic **tableau,** two actors (soldier and devil) and one dancer (the princess). The sung word which had caused trouble in **Renard** now is eliminated. The small orchestra seated on the stage consists of seven instruments, each representing a high or a low part: clarinet, bassoon, trumpet, trombone, violin, contrabass and percussion.

The proximity to jazz is evident in the scoring as well as in the stylistic treatment of the chamber orchestra. Jazz had reached Stravinsky through Ansermet who had just returned from America. Rich in syncopations and novel instrumental effects, jazz by its very nature would interest Stravinsky the rhythmician, ready to embrace something novel above all. Indeed, none of Stravinsky's scores is so replete with obstinate syncopations as is **L'Histoire du Soldat.**

Three traits characterize this music: first, the complete departure from musical illustration; second, the linear design of autonomous instrumental parts, and third, the abandonment of Russian folklore elements. The score consists of musical numbers, each one an entity stylizing the decisive contents of the action, always on the basis of rhythm; so the numbers present the marching soldier, the dancing princess, the sarcastic and triumphant devil, or the mourning soldier by the river, or the festive reception at the court, etc. How ingenious is the idea of stylizing a love scene by two chorales instead of by the customary emotional excess in such situations. This is truly a narrative point of view and anticipates the replacement of the "moving" theatre and drama—opera, ballet—

with a static type of music as found in the oratorio.

Summarizing then, we have seen how Stravinsky made greater efforts toward the linear design of his instrumental parts; on various occasions we have stressed the significance of the chamber music parts for his large ballets; we have spoken of the undiluted naked sound, that is, the opposite of blended sonorities —as is realized without compromise for the first time in **L'Histoire du Soldat.** That which in the earlier period had been stated by means of whole groups of sonorities, now is epitomized in instrumental lines of incredible plasticity. Tiny motives and rhythms of the most diversified kind are piled upon each other as though they indicated the composer's capriciousness. It is as though lines are juxtaposed to lines presumably without consideration of harmony; sometimes there are only two or three parts. In reality the score is constructed with fastidious care for the minutest detail, however, and the lines are so exactly related to the poles of tonality that the structural entities are of utmost architectural solidity. At the same time, unheard-of demands are made on the virtuoso faculties of the players.

Furthermore, the authors, conscious of Swiss internationalism, fully realized the subject matter of this work. Stravinsky has abandoned all the little Russian trimmings and fragments which heretofore had been the basis of his melodic construction. This was a move of great impact. The composer who, as Ramuz reports, had established himself in a house at Lake Geneva as though he resided at the Moskwa, had taken the first step toward his future musical cosmopolitanism.

Of no less consequence was the definite

turn toward strict form. Of course, we must not associate this word with sonatas and fugues in the sense of academic tradition. Stravinsky, instead, feels attracted to far simpler and more plastic forms such as the march, waltz, tango, ragtime, polka and galop. Shortly before he had tried small dance forms in easy piano pieces for four hands; later he was to transform them with all the virtuosity and individuality of his instrumentation into orchestral suites. These are not, as has often been contended, experiments in musical parody, but rather significant embodiments of various musical types. Jazz, then new, also stimulated Stravinsky's imagination. He wrote a **Ragtime** for eleven instruments, also the incarnation of that type. Finally he began to take an interest in the piano. It is typical of his attitude toward this instrument (which had served so long for lyrical

94

moods, confessions and pathos) that his first solo work for that medium is the **Piano-Rag-Music,** an extremely complicated, rhythmically tough and obstinate composition.

*T*HE WAR WAS OVER. THE borders opened. Stravinsky could breathe again. At once he established contact with his old friend Diaghilev who with his troupe had been in America. From the renewed collaboration with Diaghilev **Pulcinella** originated, the first work of Stravinsky's European mentality. "A pastiche," said the critics who demanded assembly line revolutionary works from this composer. "A sacrilege," said the scholars, for they saw their Pergolesi damaged by a modern dissonance hunter.

Indeed, the creation was novel: here a great Italian musician of the past was not, as had been customary, adorned with modern color, but was so thoroughly changed that he sounded simply like contemporary music. Stravinsky had gone to work not exactly with respect, but, as he said himself, with love. And so a miracle came about: Pergolesi became Stravinsky, and yet at the same time remained Pergolesi. Stravinsky points up and rejuvenates the music of the early **settecento.** He strengthens it with his own vitality. Rhythms become poignant, melodies take on plastic design, and "clang" is made transparent. **Pulcinella** represents the victory of the intellect over temperament, the victory of moderation over "introspective romanticism," and therein André Gide sees the very essence of a classical **oeuvre.**

In addition to an enlarged chamber orchestra, the composer uses three singing parts in the original version of **Pulcinella** and the singers are seated in the orchestra. Later he re-worked the most important sections of the score into an instrumental suite which has become a favorite in the modern repertory. In accordance with the methods of the eighteenth century, the strings in **Pulcinella** are divided into a **concertino** of soloists, and **tutti,** the latter reduced in number as compared to earlier techniques.

Stravinsky temporarily had become interested in the sound of strings alone. He had composed, as early as 1914, three pieces for string quartet in which he had experimented with novel sound effects. Now he composed a Concertino in the spirit of **L'Histoire du Soldat.** This work, nowadays better known in a version for chamber orchestra, was written in Carantec, Brittany. After the war Stravinsky had left Switzerland in order to settle definitely in France. Having changed his domicile again and again, he now remained in that country until the outbreak of World War II.

It is probably not just coincidence that the first larger work concluded in the country of his choice was an **Hommage** to the greatest French composer of modern times. This is the **Symphonies d'Instruments à Vent, à la Mémoire de Claude Debussy,** a peculiar mixture of the musical substance of **Les Noces** and **L'Histoire du Soldat** for an ensemble of twenty-two winds. Sections of rhythmic incisiveness and solemn, chorale-like numbers connected with one another in clever sequences of changing meters are molded into an entity; and the magnificent work is replete with melancholy — with the score making extraordinary demands on intonation and on the flexibility of the executants. Stravinsky conjures up Russian atmosphere. It is as though in honoring Debussy, he wanted to take leave of his lost native land.

A Russian theme is the basis also of his opera **Mavra,** dedicated to the memories of Glinka, Tchaikovsky and Pushkin, three artists held in high esteem by the composer. The innocuous subject matter is taken from one of Pushkin's tales: a soldier disguises himself as a girl in order to get into a household in which his beloved is employed; while being shaved he is discovered by the suddenly returning ladies. There is hardly any action—and that again corresponds to the narrative principle Stravinsky had acknowledged in his preceding works, and which he now applied to **opera buffa.** The score is a suite of strict musical forms, not excluding the waltz, a veritable compendium of humor and caprice, and bursting with refreshing hilarity.

The essence of this masterwork, which is heard too rarely, cannot better be characterized than by Stravinsky's own words as he describes **Mavra** in his **Poetics:** "My opera **Mavra** was born of a natural sympathy for the body of melodic tendencies, for the vocal style and conventional language which I came to admire more and more in the old Russo-Italian opera. This sympathy guided me quite naturally along the path of a tradition that seemed to be lost at the moment when the attention of musical circles was turned entirely towards the music drama.

"The music of **Mavra** stays within the tradition of Glinka and Dargomirsky. I had not the slightest intention of reestablishing this tradition. I simply wanted in my turn to try my hand at the living form of the **opera buffa** which was so well suited to the Pushkin tale which gave me my subject. **Mavra** is dedicated to the memory of composers, not one of whom, I am sure, would have recognized as valid such a manifestation of the tradition they created, because of the novelty of the language my music speaks a hundred years after its models flourished. But I wanted to renew the style of these dialogues-in-music whose voices had been reviled and drowned out by the clang and clatter of the music drama."

The charm of **Mavra** lies to an extent in the fact that the singing parts are accompanied practically by wind instruments only, with some strings serving exclusively to support the basses and for certain lines and color nuances. The word "accompanied" is meant in its original connotation. As a rule, the winds give nothing more than rhythmic organization which, corresponding to the spirit of the old **opera buffa,** is satisfied with the simplest accents. The time of rhythmic experimentation now seems to have moved into far distance.

Stravinsky had delineated everything he had wanted to try out, and now, as always in such situations, he turns to ever new tasks. At this point we find him more intensively occupied with the problem of melody. This problem, as we will see, gradually becomes the central concern of all his art. In **Mavra** he had striven toward free melodic design for the first time. If, while so doing, some reminiscences of the syllabic vocal technique of **Les Noces** would flow from his pen, it is not astounding.

A long-harbored love for **Italianità** came to the fore. It helped to shape Stravinsky's future creations even when momentarily he seemed to feel power-fully attracted to the spirit of French classicism. The mood of the Italian and South German divertimento is revealed in the splendid **Octuor pour Instruments à Vent.** The spirit of the preclassical con-certato is conjured up in his **Concerto for Piano and Winds,** and finally the realm of the sonata à la Domenico Scarlatti is manifest in the **Sonata** and in the **Sere-nade** for piano solo.

In the **Wind Octet,** with its unusual scoring for flute, clarinet and two bas-soons, trumpets and trombones, a bril-liant symphonia and a frivolous finale are the frame for a series of variations in which a lugubrious theme is varied with all artistic virtuosity. In the variations, hilarity and seriousness are abruptly jux-taposed. At the end a **fugato** via a theme of leaping intervals leads unexpectedly into the final movement which, again most surprisingly, resolves itself into soft and solemn chords. After so much gaiety suddenly the outlook into another world is given. Contrapuntal techniques which Stravinsky employed in **L'Histoire du Soldat** are even further developed in this **Octet.** An entirely new, a typically Stravinskyan manner of working with counterpoint becomes evident, a counterpoint loose but with lines enchained in each other to the finest degree, brilliant but full of inventiveness and substance.

A completely different aspect is encountered in the **Concerto for Piano and Woodwinds** (first performed in 1924). The word "suivi" in the original, indicating the solo piano's dominating role, is not to be understood, however, in the sense of the romantic virtuoso concerto with effective sound passages, but rather in that of a fluid, motor-like concertato style as found in the concerti of Bach and Vivaldi.

The wind orchestra pompously opens with the dotted rhythms of the so-called French overture. Then the piano takes over, at first also with strict rhythmic motives but later rejoicing, as it were, in figurative play. The piano cadenza is the climax of the first movement, producing most complicated and percussive rhythmic effects.

Similar but still more brilliant in conception is the last movement; here Stravinsky uses partly jazz effects, blending them most ingeniously into the motoric flow. The middle movement contrasts a metamorphosis, à la Vivaldi, with rhapsodic and contrapuntal structures that recall the old Italian sonata.

In comparison with **Mavra** and the **Octuor,** the **Concerto** is heavier and sometimes even has a torturing character. Within the classical palette we become cognizant of violent tensions, like those

encountered in **Le Sacre** and **Les Noces.**
The tonal structure is clearly pronounced.

What Stravinsky finds important is "not new idols, but the eternal necessity of affirming the axis of our music and recognizing the existence of certain poles of attraction. Diatonic tonality is only one means of orienting music towards these poles. The function of tonality is completely subordinated to the force of attraction of the pole of sonority. All music is nothing more than a succession of impulses that converge towards a definite point of repose." Therefore his chief concern is "not so much what is known as tonality as what one might term the polar attraction of sound, of an interval, or even of a complex of tones. The sounding tone constitutes in a way the essential axis of music. Musical form would be unimaginable in the absence of elements of attraction which make up every musical organism and which are bound up with its psychology." These sentences from the **Poetics** express Stravinsky's harmonic creed.

Serge Koussevitzky, the selfless sponsor of modern and modern Russian music in particular, suggested to Stravinsky that he play the **Concerto** himself for the première (1925: world première in Paris; American première, Boston Symphony, in the same year). After some hesitation the composer consented. It was the beginning of a pianistic activity in which the composer, trained on Czerny's pedagogical masterworks, was engaged for several decades in Europe and in the United States, and with which he had greatest success.

Those who have heard him know how Stravinsky sees his own piano works: rhythmically they are of utmost incisiveness and poignancy; emotionally they are most admirably controlled but always full of spontaneous temperament and far removed from the so-called "colorful" or "well-timbred" interpretation. His suddenly awakening happiness over his own playing produced two solo compositions more pleasing in character than the grandiose **Concerto,** though no less significant: the **Sonata,** polished derivative of the **Concerto,** and the **Serenade** which, since it is actually a suite, has many passages of most precious gracefulness.

The time had come for a new major work. The opportunity was provided by the twentieth anniversary of Sergei Diaghilev's work for the stage, and the result was **Oedipus Rex.** It is the synthesis of Stravinsky's efforts in behalf of the narrative musical theater. Stravinsky's dislike of the music drama which tended toward psychological-sensual effects has been mentioned. He gives his answer to such a music drama with **Oedipus Rex,** representing it as a scenic oratorio, a distinctive new type of music. It is a sequence of rigid, practically immovable pictures which demonstrate emotional situations. Even when certain phases of the plot are being shown they appear stylized by being related rather than by being performed in actions.

The text is but a skeleton. All statements are made through music which juxtaposes, in the manner of the Baroque oratorio, arias, duets and choruses, each one a well-knit entity. Despite this undramatic sequence of scenes there is tremendous suspense culminating in the choral narrative of Jocasta's death and of Oedipus' self-destruction. This is a triumph of musical autonomy over sensuousness, sensationalism and spine-tingling. It is equally the triumph of

110

stylization over realism, and the triumph of introspectiveness over the superficiality of pathos.

Monumentality, which since the Baroque era had been lost to music, here is rediscovered. **Oedipus Rex** is not the modern imitation of Antiquity found in so many contemporary works on classical subjects, it is the re-birth of Antiquity from the spirit of our times. Stravinsky does not shy away from utilizing ideas of most variegated stylistic epochs of European music. He employs Greek Orthodox Church music as well as elements of the Verdi opera, operatic formulae of Handel and rhythmic elements from **Les Noces** (which are, however, simplified corresponding to the monumental character of the work).

The critics found the Beckmesser-like tracing of "steals" made by Stravinsky most entertaining, but they missed the point completely. They did not realize that Stravinsky had created something new and original out of the elements of European tradition. The form of the narrative musical theatre had been originated, a prototype for our epoch from Honegger to Orff. The writers in vain tried to classify trees by following botany; naturally they missed the forests.

In order to avoid any subjective emotional interpretation whatever in **Oedipus Rex,** the composer employs a dead language. Jean Daniélou translated Jean Cocteau's ingenious condensation of Sophocles' tragedy into Latin.

"Quelle joie," Stravinsky writes in **Chroniques de ma Vie,** "de composer de la musique sur un langage conventionnel, presque rituel, d'une haute tenue s'imposant d'elle-même! On ne sent plus dominé par la phrase, par le mot dans son sens propre. Coulés dans un moule

112

immuable qui assure suffisamment leur valeur expressive, ils ne réclament plus aucun commentaire. Ainsi le texte devient pour le compositeur une matière uniquement phonétique. Il pourra le décomposer à volonté et porter toute son attention sur l'élément primitif qui le compose, c'est-à-dire sur la syllabe. Cette façon de traiter le texte n'était-elle pas celle des vieux maîtres du style sévère? Telle fut aussi, pendant des siècles, vis-à-vis de la musique, l'attitude de l'Eglise qui, par ce moyen, l'empêchait de verser dans la sentimentalité et . . . dans l'individualisme." [5]

In Stravinsky's own realm **Apollon Musagètes,** the counterpart of **Oedipus Rex,** is a ballet of strictest classical proportions, choreographed by Georges Balanchine. The writer remembers that when hearing the work for the first time he was surprised by the melodic euphony of the string orchestra, because he was accustomed to hearing harsh sounds from winds and sharp articulation from everything by Stravinsky. Only today does he fully understand the timeless beauty of this work in which melody has regained its old privileges. "Under the influence of the learned intellectualism that held sway among music lovers of the serious sort, it was for a time fashionable to disdain melody," Stravinsky writes in his **Poetics.** "I am beginning to think, in full agreement with the general public, that melody must keep its place at the summit of the hierarchy of elements that make up music. Melody is the most essential of these elements."

It is apparent that Stravinsky, since his **Mavra,** strove to regain for melody its old established privileges. This does not mean, however, that he abandoned concise rhythmic structure—on the contrary it remains one of the essential ingredients of his style. According to classical practices, **Apollon** is replete with evenly flowing rhythms derived to a large extent from the dance forms of the French **grand siècle.** Even though they are subordinated to melody, they are fixed with all possible foundation and thus serve as both support and organization. It is interesting to observe how in the course of the ballet rhythmic intensity is consistently increased until it culminates in a truly "exciting" coda.

Stravinsky himself formulates the motives underlying this new composition with his usual preciseness: "Quand, dans mon admiration pour la beauté linéaire de la danse classique, je songeai à un ballet de ce genre, j'envisageai surtout ce qu'on appelle le 'ballet blanc' où se révélait à mes yeux l'essence de cet art dans toute sa pureté. A cette fin l'écriture diatonique me parut la plus appropriée, et la sobriété de ce style détermina mon point de vue sur l'ensemble instrumental dont j'allais me servir. J'écartai tout d'abord l'orchestre courant à cause de l'hétérogénéité de sa composition: groupes d'archets, de bois, de cuivres, de percussion. J'écartai aussi les ensembles d'harmonie (bois et cuivres) dont les effets sonores ont été vraiment trop exploités ces derniers temps, et je m'arrêtai aux archets.

"L'usage orchestral de ces instruments souffre depuis assez longtemps d'une déviation fort regrettable. Tantôt on leur fait soutenir des effets dynamiques, tantôt on les abaisse au rôle de simples 'colo-

ristes.' Je confesse avoir donné moi-
même dans ce travers. La destination
primordiale des instruments à archet,
déterminée par leur pays d'origine,
l'Italie, et qui consiste avant tout dans la
culture du chant, de la mélodie, a été dé-
laissée, et pour cause. . . . Un retour à
l'étude et à la culture de cet élément au
point de vue uniquement musical me
parut tout à fait opportun et même
urgent." [6]

The composer was so fascinated with
the classical ballet that he immediately
followed **Apollon** with another work of
the same genre, **Le Baiser de la Fée.** Now
he incorporated stylistic elements of the
romantic ballet of French tradition into
his project, elements which had already
been touched upon in the **Variation de
Polymnie.** The musical material utilized
was piano literature and songs of Tchaikovsky. He "orchestrated" them just

as little as he had previously orchestrated Pergolesi. He transformed them in that he stamped them with his own personality. **Le Baiser de la Fée** is Tchaikovsky seen through Stravinsky's eyes, considerably loosened up, and yet solidified in structure and elevated to the classical sphere.

In the thirties, Stravinsky rediscovered the charm of music, the gracefulness which for so long had been lost in the symphonic grandioso of massive romantic sonorities and, no less, in the lowest ebbs of the musical entertainment industry. The result? Terms such as "amiable" or "pleasing" did not meet with too much respect from serious musicians who synonymized them with trivial and sentimental. Stravinsky, however, has always kept a good sense of humor and irony. He loves sharp, sudden and biting formulations both in conversation and in music.

In the **Capriccio** and in the **Jeu de Cartes** he is at the same time humorous and graceful, ironical and lovable. And yet nothing is lost of the unanticipated sharpness of his musical formulations, for his is not a coy, but an elegant gracefulness. His amiability, with all its smooth veneer, is sparkling, brilliant, sophisticated. It never dispenses with sudden gesticulations of a violent temperament.

The **Capriccio for Piano and Orchestra** is the gay counterpart to the vigorous **Piano Concerto.** According to Baroque definition it is so constructed that heterogeneous episodes follow each other and, as Stravinsky writes, "par leur nature, impriment à la pièce le caractère capricieux dont elle tire son nom. Un compositeur dont le génie se prêtait admirablement à ce genre fut Carl Maria von Weber, et il n'est pas étonnant que, au

cours de mon travail, j'aie surtout pensé
à lui, ce prince de la musique." [7]

The **Capriccio** is a virtuoso piece, not
only for the piano, but also for the rather
large orchestra in which the strings, as
in **Pulcinella,** are divided into solo quintet
and **ripieni.** The division of the strings
into one transparent and another more
complex body allows the production of
distinctive effects; right at the beginning
of the work the possibilities are exploited
with challenging clarity. They allow the
end of the first movement to disintegrate
into the infinite, as it were. This fast
movement is an uncommonly attractive
concertato of capricious and motoric elements, of arbitrary adornments and chiv-
alric melodies which the solo instruments
throw hither and yon—comparable to the
play of equilibrists. Later, chords of
measured gravity appear around which
the solo piano plays violent octaves as

well as repetitions of a single tone, another of Stravinsky's trademarks.

The slow middle movement contrasts sustained melodies of Baroque provenience with rhapsodic figurations of the solo piano. Influences of cymbal technique are again conspicuous and the concluding **allegro capriccioso** is full of excessive humor and joyfulness, and there is an almost confusing abundance of sound pictures around which the piano plays bravura "caprioles," thus holding the parts together.

Jeu de Cartes was a commission of the American Ballet, founded in 1936. Its maître was Georges Balanchine, the great choreographer with whom Stravinsky had worked in earlier years. Today he is considered the artist who realizes Stravinsky's ballet compositions with utmost perfection. The subject of **Jeu de Cartes** is a poker game in three "deals" or rounds in which the joker constantly tries to interfere; each of the "deals" is introduced by a vigorous refrain by means of which the ballet automatically assumes rondo form.

In the first round there is charming, even sympathetic understanding between the cards until the joker comes into the game with abrupt violence, making himself felt through sharp rhythms and chords. Yet the noble cards are not disturbed and win the game. The second "deal" starts with a mysterious march, followed by variations in which Stravinsky pokes amiable fun at all the charm and gracefulness of the romantic ballet. Once more the march is sounded, whereupon the joker invades the game with boring rhythms only to withdraw at the end from the polished conversation of the other cards. In the third "deal" all cards meet in the angular and entirely unsentimental waltz, but soon they tumble over each other with a circus-like hilarity that degenerates and assumes menacing character. At this moment the refrain, in a most surprising manner, terminates the game.

Between these two gay works stand five compositions of totally different character: the **Symphonie des Psaumes,** the **Violin Concerto,** the **Duo Concertant for Violin and Piano,** the **Concerto per due pianoforti soli** and, finally, the "mélodrame" **Persephone.**

For some time Stravinsky had contemplated writing a symphony of larger proportions. Of course he thought not of the monstrous symphonic form as developed in the nineteenth century, but interpreted the word "sin-fonia" in the original sense as an event, a tonal "happening" of periodic organization. Therefore he did not work with thematic complexes which would be segmented, worked out and developed, but chose autonomous structures to be ordered according to principles of analogy. Stravinsky possibly was inspired to use a chorus, in Latin, in his new symphony, due to previous intensive occupation with the chorus problem in **Oedipus Rex.** The motivation for the **Symphonie des Psaumes** was a commission to write a composition for the fiftieth anniversary of the famous Boston Symphony Orchestra (1930). In the **Symphonie des Psaumes,** Stravinsky, for the last time in a long period, once more manifests his predilection for the wind orchestra. He contrasts the chorus, of four parts, with an immense apparatus: five woodwind parts, a strong brass section including tromba piccola, percussion, harp and two pianos. Cellos and contrabasses again serve to intensify the bass. One could call the **Symphonie**

des Psaumes the quintessence of Stravinsky's choric enterprises after **Les Noces.** Here again the foundation is the Russian mood. The work, however, no longer exploits folklore, which Stravinsky had laid aside for some time, but rather the chanting of the Greek Orthodox liturgy. The deeply pious composer may have been led to such chanting by the verses of the Psalms which he uses in the Vulgate version.

The first part is a short prayer, the second is an artistic and complicated double fugue testifying to his increased interest in strict counterpoint; and the last and most extensive part, as the text says, sings the praise of God with psalter and harp, with timpani and dancing. Perhaps childhood memories are captured in this truly powerful piece whose solemn choral settings are strangely interrupted by unanticipatedly shocking instrumental episodes. These abrupt contrasts produce extraordinary effects. There is also, particularly in the first and last movements of the **Symphonie des Psaumes,** a clear distinction between orchestral and choral treatment; while, with the exception of the fugue, the chorus part is set primarily in chords and is articulated syllabically, the winds are given brilliant virtuoso treatment.

Persephone demonstrates a completely different aspect of Stravinsky's writing. The poem is an early work of André Gide. The construction of the **epos** is in three **tableaux** commented upon by the seer Eumolpe, a conception of theatre thoroughly corresponding to Stravinsky's own. The subject is the well-known myth of the goddess of spring, Persephone, who is stolen by Hades so she can bring a ray of eternal light into the world of the deceased. She returns to earth again so that a new spring may break forth. The strict formalism of this poem, replete with metaphors from the realm of the "Parnassien" poets, fascinated Stravinsky. Here he is not as much interested in a portrayal or a dramatic condensation of the events as in the arrangement of musical forms, the basis of which is, at least in part, a highly individualized syllabic distribution of the verses.

Of **Persephone** he writes: "J'avais toujours redouté les difficultés de la prosodie française. Quoique vivant déjà depuis bien des années dans ce pays et en parlant la langue dès mon enfance, j'avais jusqu'alors hésité à l'employer dans ma musique. Cette fois-ci je me décidai à tenter l'aventure et au cours de mon travail j'y pris de plus en plus de plaisir. Ce que je goûtais surtout, c'était d'appliquer le chant syllabique à la langue française, comme je l'avais fait déjà, pour le russe,

dans **Les Noces** et, dans **Oedipus Rex,**
pour le latin." [8]

The vocal means, chorus, speaking
voice (Persephone) and tenor solo (Eumolpe) are contrasted with a larger orchestral apparatus than Stravinsky had
used for a long time; but it is typical of
his manner of writing, becoming gradually lighter and more translucent, that
throughout the work the instruments appear prominent in solo groups which are
sometimes most unconventional combinations. It is interesting to discern how
admirably Stravinsky transforms the
spirit of French classicism into his own
ideas of sonority.

Stravinsky's title, "mélodrame," is not
to be interpreted in the obvious meaning
of a dramatic recitation with an illustrat-
ing orchestra; it is meant in the original
connotation of the word, a union of recitation and music. One would think that

a composer invariably interested in precise statements of his intentions would not care too much for the uncontrolled combination of spoken words with music. For that reason the speaking role actually is not extensive.

A mixture of scenic oratorio and classic ballet pantomime—that is **Persephone;** and its special character results from the fact that it was commissioned, in 1932, by Ida Rubinstein, both a dancer and an actress and, above all, one of the greatest sponsors of modern music. This is the one time in the recent history of the arts that an **artist** could commission such major figures as Debussy, Ravel, Honegger and Stravinsky. All were inspired by this unusual woman, for whom Ravel created his **Bolero.**

In the 1930's Stravinsky was celebrated in all musical cities of Europe and the United States as a pianist and conductor.

This performing activity took a great deal of his time, but it was the basis of his and his large family's financial existence. Stravinsky frequently found that his music came to his listeners distorted because of the lack of understanding or vanity of its interpreters, particularly the conductors, the prima donnas of the twentieth century. In comparison with the excesses and self-glorification of these maestros, even the prima donnas of the Baroque period seemed innocent young ladies. Naturally there are the glorious exceptions of Arturo Toscanini, Otto Klemperer, Hans Rosbaud and Dimitri Mitropoulos.

"The sin against the spirit of the work always begins with the sin against its letter and leads to the endless follies which an ever-flourishing literature in the worst taste does its best to sanction," writes Stravinsky in a passage of his

Poetics devoted to the description of performances of music. In performances which he himself conducted or in which he played, both in public concerts and in recording studios, Stravinsky demonstrated with convincing authority how he wanted to have his music performed.

During one of his numerous concert tours, Stravinsky became acquainted through his German publisher Willy Strecker with the young American violinist Samuel Dushkin. He at once projected the writing of a violin concerto for him. Despite his rich experience, this was a new task: the concern with the technique of the violin as a solo instrument. He went to work not without hesitation because he himself did not play the violin. Paul Hindemith gave him courage, saying that the fact that Stravinsky did not play the violin himself would be an asset . . . "que ce fait contribuerait précisément à me faire éviter une technique routinière et donnerait naissance à des idées qui ne seraient pas suggérées par le mouvement accoûtumé des doigts."[9]

Technically speaking, that work developed the violinistic manner previously applied in **L'Histoire du Soldat:** many double stops, even in the **cantabile** parts, wide skips, tone repetitions, rushing runs and violent **pizzicati** chords. Musically speaking, in the first and last movements "motorism" seems expanded in a virtuoso-like manner, and yet is traceable to Baroque music, and it is enriched toward the end by all sorts of rhythmic effects. Of the two arias, the first has a fantastic, mysterious quality with certain elements of **Jeu de Cartes** varied and deepened, while the second, in substance the highlight of the concerto, is the metamorphosis from a **cantilena** à la Bach to the musical orbit of Stravinsky.

Experience gained in the writing of the **Violin Concerto** was immediately applied to the realm of chamber music in the **Duo Concertant** for violin and piano. And here, too, an unusual arrangement is found, that of three motor-like and two cantabile movements. Titles evoke the sphere of the suite: Cantilène (incidentally as a composition of motion), Eclogue I and II, Gigue and Dithyrambe. Eclogue II and Dithyrambe are among the melodically most intensive and most suspenseful pieces Stravinsky has ever written. Just as in the solo sonata, the piano part is kept primarily in two parts and is transparent, yet at the same time strangely exciting. In the Cantilène Stravinsky works with the cymbal sounds occasionally heard in the **Capriccio.** The only explanation for the fact that this significant work has not become better known is probably the well-known indifference of our performers and of audiences of today's concert halls.

Stravinsky's second son, Soulima, had developed into a solid pianist. What, then, was more logical than penning a composition in which both father and son could be heard? That is the motivation for the magnificent **Concerto for Two Pianos** (1935). Motor ideas, experiences from earlier works and novel sound combinations, complex figurations and hammering percussive effects, virtuoso play and polyphonic constructions are unified through Stravinsky's organizing power. There are, to be sure, certain graceful moments in this work, as in the Nocturne and in the theme of the Variations. However, they are in the minority and contrast with an audacity both of thought and sound which was unexpected after

Stravinsky's immediately preceding works.

Stravinsky **is** unpredictable; even the mature artist seems always to look for something new. His artistic decisions never can be anticipated. Only today as we know the surprising development of the septuagenarian, as we see him incessantly searching for strict polyphonic solutions which would eliminate everything ornamental and almost all sensuousness of sound, can we recognize the full meaning of the **Concerto for Two Pianos.** Despite the multiplicity of sound combinations, one impression remains: condensation of thought and absoluteness of construction. Thus the technically most difficult work is concluded, logically, by a four part fugue whose hard-driven subject seems to have converted all the energies of the younger Stravinsky into polyphonic substance. What an ingenious idea—that of pushing forward the entire fugal exposition, even at the inversion of the theme, through a steady repetition of single tones!

In the succeeding work none of the artistic problems of the double concerto is felt. The **Dumbarton Oaks Concerto,** for chamber orchestra, is a vivid piece of music, one that comes from the domain of Bach's **Brandenburg Concerti.** The polyphonic profile alone of the parts hints at the new ideas Stravinsky entertains. As one studies the score more carefully, one discovers a condensation of motives —a new Stravinsky! Each one of the three movements is developed from a small intervallic step with utterly logical sequence. It is exactly this self-imposed limitation of the constructivist which reveals his inexhaustible imagination and power of combination; it reveals no less his realization of sound. **Dumbarton Oaks** radiates that feeling of well-being and dynamic repose which, in Stravinsky's own words, should be the response of listeners to all his music.

That feeling is reflected in the serenade-like middle movement with its concerted play of solo winds and strings, in which each tone is of weight and consequence despite its preciousness, but it holds true no less for the first and last movements. The first movement of the **Dumbarton Oaks Concerto** derives from the E flat major chord played up emphatically, a play with sonorities that is of most vivid gaiety, although complicated by rhythmic intricacies. In the last movement the rhythmic element is made still more emphatic; at times reigning almost with the exclusivity of the youthful works of the master, it appears, on the other hand, controlled by classical regulations. Most surprisingly, **Un Sou-**

venir d'Italie is heard, and no less unexpectedly in the middle movement there
are reminiscences of a Russian balalaika
orchestra. It is only at the end that the
chamber orchestra assumes its full sound,
in an E flat major development which
extends over several pages of the score,
and that development may be considered
a prototype of the polar "radiation" of
a chord.

$\mathcal{S}$INCE THE END OF THE 1920'S the music world of the United States had exercised an ever-increased influence on Stravinsky's composition and financial status. Famous American orchestras and American artists or music lovers had commissioned him. Many of the master's old and new friends lived in the United States. At the beginning of World War II Stravinsky had lost his wife, his oldest daughter and his mother in Paris. Shortly thereafter he settled in the

States. Among other reasons was an invitation extended by Harvard University for a series of guest lectures. These were later published under the title **Poetics of Music.**

Providence kept the terrors of another European war from him: the master who in France had matured into a "citizen of the world of music" carried the intellectual mission of Europe to the land of the future. After the War, he became an American citizen. He married Vera Soudeikine, a friend whom he had known for decades.

It is not possible to speak of an "American period" in Stravinsky's composition —at least not in the sense of his Russian and French periods. In efforts extended over several decades he had fixed on a classical approach and the autonomy of musical means in a complex but definitive way. All Stravinsky wrote in America would be unthinkable without the preceding works. Some of his new compositions have an undeniable relationship with his earlier works. For instance, the charming **Circus Polka,** composed for the Ringling Brothers - Barnum and Bailey Circus, resembles the small orchestral suites as much as the **Danses Concertantes** show a similarity to **Jeu de Cartes,** and **Dumbarton Oaks** or **Orpheus** to **Apollon.** Even where Stravinsky does propose new types, as in the two symphonies or in **The Rake's Progress,** there are close relations with earlier works.

A different atmosphere reigns in his music of the last fifteen years. It seems as though Stravinsky surveys everything he had hitherto thought and invented from a higher level. No longer does he solve one single problem at a time, but always a number of them, and he amalgamates elements of contrast into intellectual entities. In that way one must understand that Stravinsky in his more recent works applies certain elements also of the dodecaphonic technique—in his own way, to be sure. He now has absorbed and elaborated on practically everything Western musical genius had produced. With the perspective of the mature artist Stravinsky makes all these elements his own for, transformed by him, they become his original possessions. Perhaps this happens for the last time in the history of our art. Be that as it may, it does happen on a level which no other musician of our epoch has attained. We can express the quintessence of Stravinsky's mature work in three terms: **universalitas, serenitas, humanitas.** Perhaps it is symbolic that he could fulfill his human mission only at a distance from the European continent to which he belongs with all the fibres of his heart.

In the United States, five major works originated: two symphonies, the ballet **Orpheus,** the Mass, and the opera **The Rake's Progress.** It can easily be understood that a composer whose mission is geared for absolute autonomy of musical composition one day would feel the intense desire to compose a symphony. Let us remember all we have previously said, while discussing the **Symphonie des Psaumes,** about Stravinsky's conception of a symphony, its organization, structure and contents. To him a symphony was not an outlet for emotional confessions translated into music, but simply a "symphony = sounding together," combinations of tone thoughtfully organized. We know of his admiration for Johannes Brahms, the only romanticist who still remembered the original meaning of the word "sym-phony."

We also know that Stravinsky bears

no less love for Joseph Haydn. Of all masters of the past, Haydn is the one to whom he always has felt closest intellectual kinship. It is Haydn's mentality, then, which we encounter in the Stravinskyan language of the **Symphony in C,** written for the Chicago Symphony Orchestra in 1940. With respect to this work Stravinsky is supposed to have spoken of the "economized Haydn." The orchestra in the classical scoring of Beethoven here is utilized not in that traditional complexity and fullness of sound, but rather it is split up into changing passages of chamber-music-like scoring, indeed into those of solo treatment.

This technique gives the work a character of a **concertato** that is particularly strong in the two middle movements: a **Larghetto** in which finely chiselled melodies for the winds alternate with violent or even menacing parts of the strings, almost without transition; and an **Allegretto** of dance-like freshness which, taking the audience possibly by surprise, makes a transition into a **Fugato** and concludes in a dignified, elegant **Concertino** of two trumpets and three horns. There are abrupt contrasts of light and dark, of melodic gracefulness and rhythmic severity—all characteristic of the entire work. The double-faced play of smile and threat culminates almost in a conflict in the **Finale,** only to resolve itself eventually into ethereal chorale chords.

Such sequence of movements corresponds to classical order. In the outside movements the classical principle of exposition, development and recapitulation is recognizable, whereby development is not to be interpreted as "thematic workmanship" in the old sense, but rather consists of the organization oi certain motives, clever as well as temperamental. These motives are all derived from the two intervals with which the symphony commences: minor second and fourth. Gradually from this motival tension B natural, C, G, there is obtained a harmonic tension — that of tonic-dominant and, correspondingly, the first movement has a more jovial quality, while the **Finale** is pronouncedly excited. The latent tension is not resolved until the resounding final chords in which C major and G major penetrate one another in static "sound" columns. This is indeed a masterpiece of logical construction.

The **Symphony in Three Movements,** composed seven years later for the New York Philharmonic-Symphony Orchestra, was aptly called by Alexandre Tansman the sum total of Stravinsky's entire compositional effort. Indeed, all phases of his artistic development here are condensed, as it were, in a masterly manner on a new level of wisdom. The grandiose complexes of sonorities with the rhythmic harshness of **Le Sacre du Printemps** are found, as well as the graceful and elegant structures with smiling glances at Rossini. There are passages in which the orchestra is given an opportunity to demonstrate its full splendor, and there are contrapuntal **intermezzi** in which the solo instruments are combined for the linear play of ever-changing moods.

We have intentionally chosen the word **intermezzi** because, while Stravinsky in the **C major Symphony** adheres to classical structure, we find in the later work chamber-music-like **intermezzi** between exposition and recapitulation; they substitute for a "development." Only exact study of the score will fully reveal the inventiveness concealed in these **intermezzi** of the first and third movements.

147

Most surprising, at least as regards the acoustical impression, is the **Fugato** just before the end of the composition. After a powerful display of sonority by the entire orchestra, solo trombone and solo piano begin an imitative play built on major and minor seconds. Despite the acerbity of the contrapuntal technique, everything is completely undogmatic and constitutes a challenge to academic tradition. Stravinsky surprises with clever new ideas where most composers would begin elaboration.

The harmonic principle of bi-tonality as found in the **Sacre** is resumed, and with even greater logic. Harmonically, this symphony is based upon the leading-tone-tension between the poles G (C) and A flat (D flat), both in horizontal and vertical development. This tension created by the "leading tone" is fixed by a grandiose gesture in sound at the very beginning — and it is delineated with typically Stravinskyan inexorability. In the virtuoso elegance of the middle movement, as well as in the **Finale,** the minor second interval, leading tone-tonic, is interpreted for the harmonization of a triad both in major and minor.

These are perhaps too technical comments; nevertheless they seem necessary to explain the essence of an autonomous work of musical art. Likewise, one can hardly explain a literary work without some reference to sentence structure. Nor can one comprehend the beauties of painting and architecture without the knowledge of construction, or at least one can comprehend them but superficially. One should make the effort to penetrate the structure of a musical work so as to absorb its essence. Without such an effort, one may be sympathetically moved by the appearance, the sound as such —

and of course legitimately so — but one will find no admission to the technique of combination, the truly creative element in Stravinsky, an element which he himself calls "creating order." That part will remain unknown to such a listener, as it would remain hidden in the case of Bach, Brahms and Haydn.

The **Symphony in Three Movements** is surrounded by several other orchestral works for smaller combinations to which the master had felt attracted for some time because they appeared to him most suitable for the realization of his ideals relative to plastic design. Of these, the **Danses Concertantes,** originally planned as concert music, was destined for the dance stage; the **Ebony Concerto,** written for Woody Herman's well known band, is in the manner of a **Brandenburg Concerto** for jazz ensemble; and the **Concerto for String Orchestra** was dedicated, in 1946, to the twentieth anniversary celebration of the Basel Chamber Orchestra and its conductor Paul Sacher, to whom modern music owes so much. These three works, each in its own way, summarize early experiences and are representative of the mature artist. A new tone reigns in the **Ode** written in memory of Natalie Koussevitzky, the great conductor's wife who died during the war. This "elegiacal chant in three parts" for chamber orchestra was given its première by the Boston Symphony Orchestra on October 8, 1943. It foreshadows the most recent works of Stravinsky in its intellectualized structural design and in its quasi-unreal transparency of sonority.

That an artist who had developed ballet music into an autonomous concerted form would obtain commissions for the writing of dance scores is understandable; nor was it surprising that they came from America. Stravinsky's predilection for the circus and music hall is well known. It is no wonder, therefore, that he was attracted to the writing of music even for Broadway shows, so popular with Americans. The result is the **Scènes de Ballet,** composed in 1944 for Billy Rose's **Seven Lively Arts** and danced by Alicia Markova and Anton Dolin. This magnificent composition testifies to Stravinsky's sense of vitality and reality—despite his intensive occupation with the scientific and technical problems of music—and, as well, to that persuasiveness of melody which had characterized his earlier Russian works.

By no means lost, Stravinsky's old love for the romantic ballet once more comes to the fore; and again he lends new brilliance to the conventional forms by means of rhythmic ingenuity and artistry in construction and scoring. Just as in decades past, he shies away neither from trivialities nor from sentimentality; to him they are but material of sound which his intellect must transform. Stravinsky can write anything, even functional music for Broadway, and he still remains Stravinsky. That frightened Billy Rose, who suggested to the master that he have his score "gone over" by an experienced Broadway arranger in order to make it more "effective." Stravinsky was satisfied, however, with the amount of brilliance that he himself had been able to give to his music.

These were just episodes beside the grandeur of the two symphonies. Three new more significant works were ripening in him. The first is **Orpheus,** a ballet in three scenes, completed in 1946, first performance, New York, in 1948, and choreographed by Georges Balanchine. It is Stravinsky's latest contribution to the mental reconquest of Antiquity and, at the same time, it is the purest and most successful. It seems as though the Metopes of Selinunte had become sonority. This amalgamation of gracefulness and grandeur, of monumentality and penetrating gesture, of elegance and acerbity, and of suspense and release is unique! It is easily understood that Stravinsky would not use the Orpheus in the Baroque disguise with a happy ending, but in the original version which contrasts the lyricism of Orpheus and Eurydice with the brutality of the bacchantes. Orpheus is lacerated by them after he has broken his word and, upon the return from Hades, has torn the blindfold from his eyes in order to see Eurydice. Apollo appears, seizes the harp of Orpheus, and raises his chant toward heaven.

The structural organization corresponds to the strict rules of the classical ballet: **airs de danse, pas des Furies, pas de deux, pas d'action.** They furnish the excuse for the composer's construction of musical forms. They are even richer and more complex than those of **Apollon Musagètes.** The basic mood of the music is more serious and restrained, but nevertheless it displays a wealth of musical sonorities in which the contents of each scene are stylized simply and conclusively. There is a hymn-like tenderness in the musical numbers with which the ballet opens and concludes. There are string chords and three-part scoring for horns, based on solemnly progressing tones of the harp. That instrument is used as a melody bearer as it had been employed in the **Symphony in Three Movements.**

There is utmost gracefulness in the audaciously contrived linearity of the solo instruments, and there is exciting and at the same time well controlled movement in the **pas des Furies,** stylized particularly in the strings. Dignified melodies of Baroque, and yet again of modern coinage are found in the scenes between Orpheus and Eurydice. It was indeed a glorious idea to silence the string orchestra for one entire measure when Orpheus tears off his blindfold: it is the echo of Mozart's technique of introverted drama. There are dense polyphonic movements of threatening earnestness, and finally there is the mysterious eruption of elemental powers as the bacchantes tear Orpheus to pieces—that is the only moment in which the full orchestra is at work.

Stylistically speaking, there are — in addition to the formulae of the late Baroque and romantic eras frequently employed by Stravinsky — influences also of Monteverdi, for the first time, and even of medieval composers. Stravinsky's historical perspective appears ever more expanded. His knowledge now embraces **all** traditions; his personality can unify these traditions into **original** works of art. This autonomous work **Orpheus** — therein lies perhaps Stravinsky's greatest secret — is a ballet of subtlest concreteness of sound gesture. Plasticity of dance and pantomime have gained by the concentration on the absolutely necessary.

What could have persuaded Stravinsky to spend precious years on the composition of an opera? He is, after all, not a mime and not a dramatist. The essence of the dramatic is foreign to an artist of his esthetic ideals. In fact he dislikes the drama: no inward restlessness for him, no conflicts pregnant with suspense and psychological interpretation, no expression of pathos per se! Yet without a doubt he has a very strong feeling for the stage, or perhaps rather for the opportunities offered to a musical mime. His only and unique relation to the stage lies therefore in the ballet. He came from the choreographic drama to the classical, strict, formal ballet, and from there conquered additional forms of the stage such as the scenic cantata, the pantomime drama, the scenic oratorio and the choreographic melodrama.

He was perhaps attracted to the opera because he wanted to contrast the customary musico-dramatic type with one purely musical—or because he attempted to find a solution in the present day confusion of operatic esthetics, a solution which in its own way was definitive and logical in the extreme. There had been no definite solution since Debussy's **Pelléas and Mélisande,** and even Richard Strauss, the greatest creator of opera in our time, had wavered between the music drama and the musical opera, the opera for musicmaking. Recent opera composers had selected elements most suited to their dramaturgical plans from the heritage of music drama and **verismo,** from the old "number opera" and choreographic pantomime.

Stravinsky's central problem lies in formal organization. For that reason only the "number opera" could attract his fancy, for it is one in which he could make music, as he said himself with respect to **The Rake's Progress.** This work then, too, is narrative theatre, a picture sequence of three times three scenes in which librettists W. H. Auden and Chester Kallman transfer Hogarth's grandiose cycle of the Rake to the operatic stage. The cycle deals with that wasteful libertine who ends in misery and poverty through his own fault.

As compared to Hogarth's character of the London picture series, the opera's Tom Rakewell, but a weak and undecided boy, acts not from his own temperament but is pushed by Nick Shadow, a Mephistophelean gentleman with buffo antics. Of what is Mr. Rakewell guilty, if in the end he is destroyed like Don Giovanni? He escapes from the Philistine provinces into the big city. He runs away from Ann, his fiancée, a provincial and sentimental girl. He throws himself, against his will and almost in disgust, into the arms of Mother Goose, the owner of a London brothel which Stravinsky strips of any sensuousness whatever. Again against his wishes, Tom marries Baba the Turk, a bearded lady of the circus. He invents a machine which by means of a wheel can transform stones into bread, a truly harmless pleasure. In order to get our good Tom into an institution in the end, there is nothing left to the authors but to take refuge in the old operatic device of the magic curse by which Tom, impoverished, becomes insane while longing for his Ann.

We must ask forgiveness for a somewhat ironic description of a libretto, the dramaturgical weaknesses of which could certainly not have escaped a man of Stravinsky's intelligence. These deficiencies interested him little, however, for the book was just pretext for writing a **bel canto** opera. **The Rake's Progress** means triumph of melody in which Stravinsky sees the vitality of musical art.

Modern music, as he saw it, had not produced a novel type of **cantabile,** therefore Stravinsky for decades had remained faithful to the art of the great Italian melodists, an art truly corresponding to his own. "Je suis le fiancé de la musique italienne," he had told Roland-Manuel as early as 1920. As a melodic work, **The Rake's Progress** is unique and simply unsurpassable.

Bright "investigators" may mark with the red pencil of their musico-historical training that this snatch is derived from Mozart, that a steal from Verdi, that this is Rossini and that Offenbach, this Weber and that Tchaikovsky — all of these musicians indeed are cited. But they must not forget that Mozart, too, as modern research has proved, used older sources as well as formulae of his own period for the basic motives of his melodies. So did Verdi. All that matters is what composers can do with borrowed snatches. Stravinsky makes Stravinsky of them. The unique vocal charm of this opera derives from the fact that the melodies always remind the listener of something seemingly known; in reality they are arbitrarily deflected also rhythmically. They betray the disgust with sentimentality which had been typical of Stravinsky from the outset.

Similar to that of **Mavra** harmony here is based mainly upon tonal chords with strangely "fluorescent" neighboring tones, steady dislocations in the metrical scheme and, last but not least, the everchanging color of instrumentation. In this complex score one will never find the regular sequence of four measure periods forming the tradition of classical construction. Syncopations, expansions, contractions and surprising changes of note values lend the superficially even flow of music a strange inner excitement.

Add to that the peculiar distribution of accents in the accompaniment which often appears as stereotyped as in old operas! Upon close inspection, however, we realize that Stravinsky always makes little changes, sometimes hardly perceptible, in both heavy and light parts of the measure, employing rests in places normally demanding accentuation, and accenting on the other hand, however light, weak measure beats. There always seems something in discordance with the customary scheme of things. Every note of the score reflects Stravinsky's original signature; he has worked it out with the artistry of a engineer whose **métier** consists of utilizing the most clever techniques and yet of knowing how to conceal them. The unheard-of wealth of in-

vention in **The Rake's Progress** is fully
revealed only under the microscope.

But in this epoch fond of superficiality
who wants to waste energy in the study
of such minute details of a musical work
of art? Today one is perhaps willing to
investigate the merely mechanical functioning of twelve-tone rows; but the exploration of how a living artistic organism functions is nothing which would
concern most critics of **The Rake's Progress.** Such exploration, of course, would
demand too great an effort. In particular
it would require empathy—a feeling for
the composer's creative fantasy and imagination.

And all that has been said about the
structure of the small forms may be applied to the construction-at-large. There
is no stereotyped scheme in the total organization, nor is there routine in the
succession of forms. With a mas-

tery veritably incomparable, Stravinsky breaks through the closed "numbers" of the works by means of small inserts, recitatives, abrupt changes of tonality or motion. Especially a large, complete "number," such as the scene of Ann's aria concluding the first act, is a prototype of his architectural artistry.

The total organization of the opera is, in accordance with the subject matter, one of steady crescendo. First there is but one vigorous accent: that picture replete with circus temperament in Mother Goose's establishment. In the second act, however, there are several climaxes: the meeting of Tom Rakewell with Ann in front of his London villa (duo); the pompous appearance of the Turkish Baba, stylized, not without irony, through solemn rhythms; and finally, the furious outburst of the clucking, chattering, proverbially stupid Baba.

The auctioning off of Rakewell's effects with which the third act begins might perhaps better be placed at the end of the second act, even though that might entail a change of proportions. This great buffo "number," including its lyrical **intermezzi,** is one of the most original sections of the opera, full of humor and wit and pregnant with bubbling vitality. From it the scene changes to the cemetery where Nick Shadow ejaculates his magical curse on the desperate Rakewell. Demoniacal operatic theatre is not exactly Stravinsky's forte. He solves that problem in his own manner. He allows the dramatic dialogue of the two actors to be accompanied only by the harpsichord while framing it with larger musical numbers. The forms are contracted in accordance with the dramatically exciting events. In the last picture, containing scenic references to sentimental operatic devices and showing the last meeting of the Rake with Ann in the asylum as well as his death, recitatives and small numbers crowd each other.

We do not share the often stated opinion that this final picture, because of its supreme emotional effectiveness, is also the musical climax of the work. We particularly admire the manner in which Stravinsky understands how to stylize musically with most economical means. The combination of shuddering naturalism and sentimentality in this scene is not close to Stravinsky's temperament. However we are charmed—and each time anew—by the Epilogue filled with that spiritual abandon which one can easily consider the purest expression of Stravinsky's mature personality.

The world première of **The Rake's Progress** took place in Venice in the autumn of 1952, and it was first performed at the Metropolitan Opera House the following February.

Preceding the opera, Stravinsky composed a most original work which stands at the beginning of the latest phase of his rich productivity: the Mass. Latest phase? For the time being, of course, because one never knows what flight direction his incessantly searching imagination will take. Just as **The Rake's Progress,** the Mass is also written on his own initiative, and that gives the work a special significance. It is beyond previous experiences. One can, for that reason, make no comparison whatever with the **Symphonie des Psaumes** for that **oeuvre** is a concert work, while Stravinsky in composing the Mass thought of its liturgical use. Therefore we find here conciseness and relative simplicity of the choral setting.

The diatonic manner of writing, which

for some time had been the label of Stravinsky's music, is here still further simplified, which, of course, does not exclude sharp clashes of sound produced primarily by the combination of the four-part chorus with an orchestra of two oboes, English horn, two bassoons and three trombones. Stylistically speaking, the Mass is based upon a strange amalgamation of syllabic choral setting with the melodies revolving around small intervals, and all belonging to the realm of Greek Orthodox chanting.

Stravinsky not only avoids any musical exegesis of the text of the Mass—which in his case is understood—but he equally avoids recitation in accordance with the meaning of language. The strange oriental impression of the music derives from the emphatic and well thought-out accentuation of the light syllables of the words, developed to the minutest detail.

Of oriental provenience also are the strange ornaments of the solo voices as they occasionally emerge from the syllabic choric articulation. In the Mass stubbornness of sonority is coupled with transcendency of sound in the most original manner. There are just a few **forte** passages. Therefore words like "Sanctus" or "ecclesiam" terrifyingly jump out of the psalmodic repose, and only once are chorus and wind instruments combined in fullblast sonority, in the Hosanna—and even there only for a few seconds.

The Mass leads directly to the most recent compositions Stravinsky has published, the **Cantata,** the **Septet,** the **Shakespeare Songs,** and **In Memoriam: Dylan Thomas.** The seventy-year-old artist now concerns himself with chamber music forms of special instrumental combinations. This turn toward concisely constructed works for but a few vocal and instrumental parts is, like everything else in Stravinsky's writing, based upon preceding development. We have already discussed his predilection for solo grouping of instruments of the orchestra. The more the "line" in music became of interest to him, the more independent became his solo parts, whether they complement each other in a virtuoso or in a polyphonic context. He no longer thinks primarily of the play with sonorities, but of the intellectual epitomization of melodic and rhythmic substances by means of linear structures.

All techniques of polyphonic imitation and canon with rhythmic abbreviations or extensions are applied, and all the devices of the dodecaphonic technique, such as inversion and **cancrizans,** are utilized, and at the same time such devices are captured in a light and loose context of sound. Actually few listeners will hear all that is concealed in these scores in the way of inventiveness, power of combination and mastery in construction.

In contrast to many a young composer who, following von Webern, is so absorbed in the perfect functioning of his series that he forgets the sound, or at least melody and rhythm, Stravinsky is always and above all the musician. He knows that melody must not cease to play the dominating role in a symphony. He is well aware of the fact that a musical form cannot exist without a clear rhythmic organization perceptible to the ear. Perhaps this is the most admirable aspect of the most recent works of the master. He knows how to combine extreme poly-melodic and poly-rhythmic contexts with the plasticity and logic of musical sound. Of course, one must not think of more or less artificial acoustical sensation in this respect, but rather of the sound ideal of the mature Bach or that of medieval masters.

It is absolutely commensurate with Stravinsky's most recent efforts that in an ever-increased manner he would utilize—for instance in the **Septet** and **In Memoriam**—rows (series) in the manner of the twelve-tone technique. Whenever he does, he does not work with that technique dogmatically, and frequently he is satisfied with a series of eight tones or less which, even if they do include several chromatic steps, are always related in their compositional basis of reference to poles of tonality. As a matter of fact, the tonality references of an entire composition are particularly clearly pronounced in his latest works. There is no doubt that Stravinsky in this blend of tonality and "reduced" technique of series has advanced music, that he has

174

made a step of historical importance offering an "exit" from the confusion prevalent today.

The **Cantata** is for soprano, tenor, women's chorus and an instrumental ensemble of two flutes, oboe, English horn and cello. The poems are anonymous, from the fifteenth and sixteenth centuries. Between a four-times repeated, very simple, dirge-like refrain of the chorus we find a **ricercare** for soprano solo and tenor solo plus a duo of the two soloists, "Western Wind," the nervous excitement of which forms the most surprising contrast to the calm restraint of the rest of the **Cantata.** The **Septet** for clarinet, horn, bassoon, piano, violin, viola and cello is in three movements. A **concertante** movement is succeeded by an ascetic **passacaglia,** the theme of which is transformed into an extremely artistic **gigue** with reference to a series.

The three **Shakespeare Songs,** for mezzo soprano, flute, clarinet and viola, join the eighth sonnet of the English poet with two brief fragments from **The Tempest** and **Love's Labour's Lost.** Strongly linear treatment in four part writing is juxtaposed to the Stravinskyan brand of transparent sound, but so that even the descriptive associations are captured including all their poetical meaning, like the "ding-dong" of the bell of the water nymphs and the cuckoo call so beloved in old music. There are no hollow abstractions, and sonority is again the alpha and omega of this music which represents the intellectual epitomization of Stravinsky's late style.

In Memoriam: Dylan Thomas was written by Stravinsky in memory of the young English poet who died recently under tragic circumstances. The juxtaposition of tenor solo, four trombones and solo string quartet is reminiscent of the Ars Antiqua of the thirteenth century, and Stravinsky's music reawakens its spirit of pedestrian-like acerbity; two canons frame a new canon, a song for the tenor accompanied only by strings. The melody of this song is of purely instrumental character. The composition has for its basis a series composed of but a few tones; the row consists of major and minor seconds and a minor third. The result is a chromatic character, more particularly a static chromaticism plus plastic melodic design, almost the opposite of von Webern's aphoristic expressionism.

In the most recent works Stravinsky uses a minimum of orchestral means and sound material in order to obtain the utmost in logical construction and factual statement. With such minimum he achieves a maximum of intellectual concentration, the phenomenon of music per se and, at the same time, the substratum of Western musical thinking.

Our brief commentary on the most recent phase of Stravinsky's composition may be most aptly concluded by some sentences which the reader will find at the end of the third chapter of his **Poetics:** "The creator's function is to sift the elements he receives from the imagination, for human activity must impose limits upon itself. The more art is controlled, limited, worked over, the more it is free. As for myself, I experience a sort of terror when, at the moment of setting to work and finding myself before the infinitude of possibilities that present themselves, I have the feeling that everything is permissible to me. If everything is permissible to me, the best and the worst; if nothing offers me any resistance then any effort is inconceivable, and I cannot use anything as a basis, and consequently every undertaking becomes futile.

"What delivers me from the anguish into which an unrestricted freedom plunges me is the fact that I am always able to turn immediately to the concrete things that are here in question. I have no use for a theoretic freedom. Let me have something finite, definite — matter that can lend itself to my operation only insofar as it is commensurate with my possibilities. And such matter presents itself to me together with its limitations. I must in turn impose mine upon it. So here we are, whether we like it or not, in the realm of necessity. And yet which of us has ever heard talk of art as other than a realm of freedom? This sort of heresy is uniformly widespread because it is imagined that art is outside the bounds of ordinary activity. Well, in art as in everything else, one can build only upon a resisting foundation: whatever constantly gives way to pressure, constantly renders movement impossible. My freedom thus consists in my moving about within the narrow frame that I have assigned myself for each one of my undertakings.

"I shall go even further: my freedom will be so much the greater and more meaningful the more narrowly I limit my field of action and the more I surround myself with obstacles. Whatever diminishes constraint, diminishes strength. The more constraints one imposes, the more one frees one's self of the chains that shackle the spirit."

The French quotations, used with permission
of the publishers, are from:

CHRONIQUES DE MA VIE

by Igor Stravinsky
Denoël et Steele, Paris, 1935.

The English quotations, used with permission
of the publishers, are from:

POETICS OF MUSIC

In The Form of Six Lessons
by Igor Stravinsky
Translated by Arthur Knodel and Ingolf Dahl
Harvard University Press, Cambridge, 1947.

181

APPENDIX

1) *"Expression has never been an inherent property of music. That is by no means the purpose of its existence. If, as is nearly always the case, music appears to express something, this is only an illusion and not a reality. It is simply an additional attribute which, by tacit and inveterate agreement, we have lent it, thrust upon it, as a label, a convention—in short, an aspect which, unconsciously or by force of habit, we have come to confuse with its essential being."*

2) *"a driving-force in every kind of human activity, and is in no wise peculiar to artists. But that force is only brought into action by an effort, and that effort is work."*

3) *"Before tackling the* Sacre du Printemps, *which would be a long and difficult task, I wanted to refresh myself by composing an orchestral piece in which the piano would play the most important part—a sort of* Konzertstück. *In composing the music, I had in my mind a distinct picture of a puppet, suddenly endowed with life, exasperating the patience of the orchestra with diabolical cascades of arpeggi. The orchestra in turn retaliates with menacing trumpet-blasts. The outcome is a terrific noise which reaches its climax and ends in the sorrowful and querulous collapse of the poor puppet. Having finished this bizarre piece, I struggled for hours, while walking beside Lake Geneva, to find a title which would express in a word the character of my music and consequently the personality of this creature.*

"One day I leapt for joy. I had indeed found my title— Petrouchka, *the immortal and unhappy hero of every fair in all countries."*

4) *"What fascinated me in this verse was not so much the stories, which were often crude, nor the pictures and metaphors, always so deliciously unexpected, as the sequence of the words and syllables, and the cadence they create, which produces an effect on one's sensibility very closely akin to that of music."*

5) *"What a joy it is to compose music to a language of convention, almost of ritual, the very nature of which imposes a lofty dignity! One no longer feels dominated by the phrase, the literal meaning of the words. Cast in an immutable mold which adequately expresses their value, they do not require any further commentary. The text thus becomes purely phonetic material for the composer. He can dissect it at will and concentrate all his attention on its primary constituent element—that is to say, on the syllable. Was not this method of treating the text that of*

183

the old masters of austere style? This, too, has for centuries been the Church's attitude towards music, and has prevented it from falling into sentimentalism, and consequently into individualism."

6) "When, in my admiration for the beauty of line in classical dancing, I dreamed of a ballet of this kind, I had specially in my thoughts what is known as the 'white ballet,' in which to my mind the very essence of this art reveals itself in all its purity. I found that the absence of many-colored effects and of all superfluities produced a wonderful freshness. This inspired me to write music of an analogous character. It seemed to me that diatonic composition was the most appropriate for this purpose, and the austerity of its style determined what my instrumental ensemble must be. I at once set aside the ordinary orchestra because of its heterogeneity, with its groups of string, wood, brass, and percussion instruments. I also discarded ensembles of wood and brass, the effects of which have really been too much exploited of late, and I chose strings.

"The orchestral use of strings has for some time suffered a sad falling off. Sometimes they are destined to support dynamic effects, sometimes reduced to a role of simple "colorists." I plead guilty myself in this respect. The original purpose of strings was determined in the country of their origin—Italy—and was first and foremost the cultivation of canto, of melody; but this, for good reasons, has been abandoned. . . . It seemed to me that it was not only timely but urgent to turn once more to the cultivation of this element from a purely musical point of view."

7) "by their very nature give the piece that aspect of caprice from which it takes its name.

"There is little wonder that, while working at my Capriccio, I should find my thoughts dominated by that prince of music, Carl Maria von Weber, whose genius admirably lent itself to this manner. Alas! no one thought of calling him a prince in his lifetime!"

8) "I had always been afraid of the difficulties of French prosody. Although I had been living in France for twenty years, and had spoken the language from childhood, I had until now hesitated to use it in my music. I now decided to try my hand, and was more and more pleased as my work proceeded. What I most enjoyed was syllabifying the music to French as I had done for Russian in Les Noces, and for Latin in Oedipus Rex."

9) "as it would make me avoid a routine technique, and would give rise to ideas which would not be suggested by the familiar movement of the fingers."